When the
HEAVENS
are
BRASS

Keys to Genuine Revival

John Kilpatrick

Revival Press

An Imprint of
Destiny Image® Publishers, Inc.
P.O. Box 310
Shippensburg, PA 17257-0310

ISBN 1-56043-190-3

Third Printing: 1997   Fourth Printing: 1997

For Worldwide Distribution
Printed in the U.S.A.

This book and all other Destiny Image, Revival Press, and Treasure House books are available at Christian bookstores and distributors worldwide.

For a U.S. bookstore nearest you, call **1-800-722-6774**.
For more information on foreign distributors, call **717-532-3040**.
Or reach us on the Internet: **http://www.reapernet.com**

Acknowledgments

Revival is here, my friend. As a pastor, one of the places I see it most clearly is in the diligence of faithful workers under what most people would consider to be impossible circumstances. Revival only comes where unity in the Spirit is found. Most people who hear of this revival think of me, of Evangelist Stephen Hill, or of Lindell Cooley, our worship leader. It is our faces that are most often seen on the platform in our revival services, in magazine articles, and in videotapes, but the truth is that it takes the cooperation and dedicated efforts of hundreds of people to take care of the hard labor of practical ministry that is necessary for our meetings. It is the diligent labor of many unseen and often unthanked servants of God that opens the door for the Holy Spirit to move so freely among the people in each service without distraction.

Each time I see Rose Compton in the congregation, I wonder what I would do without such an able administrative assistant. Who else could work so well and so smoothly with the more than 350 trained workers who so faithfully serve on our prayer teams night after night? Every time I glance to my left, I see Bill Bush, the head usher who, with his wife Jeanie, volunteers countless hours coordinating 75 of the most outstanding ushers I have ever known. Night after night, Steve Whitehead and his loyal crew of cameramen and technicians amaze me; thanks to them, every moment of the revival is captured on videotape and audiotape. Our security team and volunteer plainclothes police officers help to meet the safety concerns of the thousands who attend the service nightly.

In the next section I see my beloved wife, Brenda. God started the revival fire in my wife of 28 years before the fire started in me; it made me jealous to go after God to get what she had. Sitting near my precious Brenda is Lila Terhune, head of our intercessors. Always faithful is the diligent R.L. Berry, our church treasurer and my trusted friend. Cheryl Grayson catches my eye in the balcony, adept in her management of our pastors' conferences. As I look at the balcony, I think of Teresa Castleman and the four deliverance teams who spend hour upon hour in personal ministry, praying for people to be set free from the bondage of past sins.

Each time I see Elmer Melton and the members of our fine Board of Directors, or any of our more than 20 deacons, I am strengthened and encouraged. I am grateful to God for people like the lovable Randy Worrel, who visits the sick and ministers to the bedridden, for our faithful interpreters for the deaf, and for Vann Lane, our dedicated and dynamic children's pastor. Joining me on the platform is our evangelist and my close friend of many years, Stephen Hill; our anointed psalmist, Lindell Cooley; the worship team; and our ever-faithful choir and orchestra. Then there is our energetic youth pastor, Richard Crisco; my trusted associate minister, Carey Robertson; my Jewish teacher and friend, Dick Reuben; and the dean of our new school, Dr. Michael Brown. When revival came to Brownsville, God did a work in all of our lives. Now we have a greater love and hunger for Him than ever before.

Contents

Foreword

John Kilpatrick has been in the pastoral ministry for more than 25 years. I have had the privilege of knowing him personally for 13 of those years. He is not only a dear friend but also a biblical pastor in the fullest sense of the word.

It is virtually impossible to plow along in the field of ministry for any period of time without experiencing major disappointment and incredible victories—and everything in between. John Kilpatrick's road to revival has been full of bends, turns, hills, stop signs, and of course, lots of traffic.

He has fought "bull" demons from hell and experienced firsthand the warfare of the enemy. Victory has come—and continues to come—with a price. William Bramwell once said, "Never look for peace while you proclaim war." John Kilpatrick has proclaimed war. He has planted his feet firmly in the trenches, vigilantly protecting his flock and fighting to the end for the salvation of souls.

This book, *When the Heavens Are Brass,* is timely. America and the world are on the verge of a widespread awakening. We need to be alerted to the fact that a price must be paid in order to break through the enemy's lines and plunder his camp. I encourage the reader to heed the words of the late Leonard Ravenhill: "Don't just go through this book, but let this book go through you."

May the Lord open the eyes of your spiritual mind and enable you to grasp the truths in this much-needed book.

Stephen Hill
Evangelist

Introduction

Corporate businessmen in expensive suits kneel and weep uncontrollably as they repent of secret sins. Drug addicts and prostitutes fall to the floor on their faces beside them, to lie prostrate before God as they confess Jesus as Lord for the first time in their lives. Reserved elderly women and weary young mothers dance unashamedly before the Lord with joy. They have been forgiven. Young children see incredible visions of Jesus, their faces a picture of divine delight framed by slender arms raised heavenward.

I see these scenes replayed week after week, and service after service. Each time, I realize that in a very real way, they are the fruit of a seven-year journey in prayer, and of two and a half years of fervent corporate intercession by the church family I pastor at Brownsville Assembly of God in Pensacola, Florida.

The souls who come to Christ, repenting and confessing their sin, the marriages that are restored, the many people who are freed from bondage that has long held them captive—these are the marks of revival and the trophies of God's glory. No, I am not speaking of a revival that lasted one glorious weekend, one week, one month, or even one year! At this writing, the "Brownsville Revival" has continued unbroken, except for brief holiday breaks, since Father's Day, June 18, 1995! How? Only God knows. Why? First, because it is God's good pleasure, and second, perhaps because the soil of our hearts was prepared in prayer long before revival descended on us so suddenly.

On that very normal and ordinary Sunday morning in June of 1995, I was scheduled to minister to my congregation, but I felt weary. I was still trying to adjust to the recent loss of my mother, and my years-long desire for revival in the church seemed that morning to be so far off. So I asked my friend, Evangelist Steve Hill, to fill the pulpit in my place. Although he was scheduled to speak only in the evening service, Steve agreed to preach the Father's Day message. We didn't know it then, but God was at work in every detail of that meeting.

The worship was ordinary (our worship leader, Lindell Cooley, was still ministering on a missions trip to the Ukraine in Russia), and even Brother Hill's message didn't seem to ignite any sparks that morning—until the noon hour struck. Then he gave an altar call and *suddenly* God visited our congregation in a way we had never experienced before. A thousand people came forward for prayer after his message. That was almost half of our congregation! We didn't know it then, but our lives were about to change in a way we could never have imagined.

We knew better than to hinder such a mighty move of God, so services just continued day after day. We had to adjust with incredible speed. During the first month of the revival, hundreds of people walked the aisles to repent of their sins. By the sixth month, thousands had responded to nightly altar calls. By the time we reached the twelfth month, 30,000 had come to the altar to repent of their sins and make Jesus Lord of their lives.

At this writing, 21 months and over 470 revival services later, more than 100,000 people have committed their lives to God in these meetings—only a portion of the 1.6 million visitors who have come from every corner of the earth to drink in of God's revival river. The local newspaper was quick to write very favorable articles about what has been called "The Brownsville Outpouring," and national Christian magazines were soon to follow suit.

Almost every month, chartered airliners filled with people who come to attend the revival from England, Canada, Norway, Germany, Japan, Korea, Scotland, New Zealand, Australia, Finland, and countless other countries land at the Pensacola airport. Many of these people arrive in Pensacola because churches in their nation pooled their resources to send representatives to Brownsville, hoping that they will bring the fire of revival back to their homeland. Our local law enforcement officials have had to make some interesting adjustments to accommodate the revival. They first noticed a difference when reports of traffic jams and erratic drivers started to filter into their stations. Now drivers who seem to be shaking or drunk while driving are commonplace. The officers who stop these drivers often wave the people on when they hear, "We've been to Brownsville" or, "Oh, it's the Lord."

Before and After

Before the revival, our church had grown to a solid congregation of nearly 2,000. We had a healthy respect for Bible preaching and godly living. A television outreach program and all the usual ministries were functioning in our fellowship. This may sound wonderful, but I wasn't satisfied. I had a deep longing in my soul for more of God's presence and power. There were still so many in this region who were far from God, and my pastor's heart burned for the many people in my own congregation who were still so bound and hindered by the enemy.

It was this longing for more that led me to a deeper journey of prayer seven years before the revival descended in June of 1995. During those early struggles, God began to instruct me through His Word about the nature of prayer, and why "the heavens were brass." Of course, many of our prayers were answered during that time, but sometimes I had to admit that the heavens seemed to be made of impenetrable brass. In the depths of my being there burned a hunger for God, for more of His holy presence, that only a feast of fire could satisfy.

Since the heavens opened and revival came, thousands of visiting pastors, evangelists, and church leaders have confessed to me that they have had the same desperate hunger for God, and they too have felt from time to time the same frustration of "brassy heavens." I am convinced that the answers I received and put into practice during my seven-year prayer journey were part of God's plan to lay a foundation in our people for revival. Revival cannot come until the heavens are made crystal clear through repentance and prayer. Revival will not come until God's people allow themselves to be changed and prepared through the discipline of fervent prayer.

Perhaps the clearest and most irrefutable proofs of true revival are the written testimonies of people whose lives have been transformed by God's power. The stories come in each week in overwhelming numbers through E-mail, faxes, and letters, bringing incredible miracles to light.

A mother reported that her oldest son and his wife are now born again. A father wrote of the conversion of his ten-year-old son. A young woman happily related how within one month of attending the revival meetings she was born again, baptized with water, filled with the Holy Spirit, and healed of a chronic infection. A respected businessman told of the brokenness that has haunted him because of early years of sexual abuse and rejoiced in the delivering power of Jesus Christ that healed him and set him forever free.

From the baptismal pool, two lesbians confessed Christ as their Lord and Savior, renounced their sin, and asked for forgiveness from the son they had raised together. The young man said to his mother, "Oh, Mom. My prayers have been answered." These two gloriously saved and delivered women immediately moved to separate living quarters. Both of these new believers work for a large corporation in the Pensacola area and are well known. Now they proclaim the gospel of their risen Lord and His power to deliver. Their testimonies have had a profound effect on those who know them.

Many reports of healing have also accompanied the revival. A young man with a pinhole in a heart valve told of his total healing. An older woman who struggled with partial hearing in her right ear for a quarter of a century was instantly and completely healed while standing in the altar area. A woman with pyelonephritis and a left kidney damaged since childhood fell under the power of God. As she lay on the carpet, she felt a popping sensation in her left side. When she finally stood up again, she was free from pain and inflammation for the first time in years! A nurse had suffered with severe lung damage for two long years. She had spent $10,000 just for her prescription drugs, not counting the other mounting medical bills. After she attended the revival meetings, the nurse returned home to her husband and children in complete health. She no longer had to depend on expensive drugs to ease her pain and help her breathe.

Another mother wrote to us to confess that she had considered suicide, but somehow, for some reason, she and her husband had attended the revival, where they came to the altar together to repent of their sins and commit their lives to Jesus. "Never in my life have I known such joy," she wrote. "I keep praising the Lord and thanking Him."

Revival Spreads

So many pastors and ministers have come to the revival that we decided to hold a semi-annual pastors' conference. Nearly 680 ministers came to the first conference, which was held in November of 1995, only five months after the revival began. The second pastors' conference, in April of 1996, ministered to nearly 1,400 registrants. The third conference, in November of that year, was flooded by 2,029 hungry, on-fire-for-God pastors from almost every denomination. Each of these conferences has helped us to see our dream come to pass—I believe it is God's dream too—as these pastors took the fire of revival home to their congregations and communities, causing the revival to explode beyond the bounds of geography, religious denomination, and nationality.

When the Heavens Are Brass

Despite the many who have been blessed by God's growing revival fire, not all have yet tasted of God's heavenly feast or stepped into His mighty river of refreshing. Some have a growing thirst for God's presence that has not been quenched. Others have rejected this fresh move of God's Spirit, as has happened so many times before in great awakenings and historical revivals. Still others have lost hope that the revival Spirit will touch them. Although the fire of revival has spread to certain churches and cities, there are far more who still struggle on under brassy heavens without a single flicker of hope for revival's fire. I can't walk away from these brothers and sisters who still stagger under the weight of the same burden I once carried. The heartbreaking telephone calls I've received from desperate pastors of declining churches, who have little faith for a breakthrough, are etched in my memory.

Why is it that the fires of revival have come to some but have not spread through this continent and the world? Perhaps you've asked this question. Indeed, you may be reading this book because you want to experience a personal Pentecost or you long to bring genuine revival to your family, your ministry, or your church. I want to share with you what I learned during the seven years before the revival came to Brownsville. Before God visited us in 1995, I had grown weary of the hype that so often floods our churches. I was tired of attending fabricated revivals that were woven together by carefully orchestrated services, being dependent more on the ability to impress and influence than on the anointing of God that is birthed only in prayer and travail.

It was during those years of spiritual hunger and searching that God opened my eyes to see why the heavens had become brass, and why revival seemed so far away. He used these many years and seasons of prayer, fasting, and longing for true revival to teach me how to pray more effectively. My congregation joined me in this pilgrimage of fervent intercession. I can tell you today with great joy that our journey in prayer has an exciting destination! The truths I learned about prayer and brass heavens laid the foundation for revival and a fresh understanding of God's *kabod*, the Hebrew term for His glory or "weightiness." The things I share have been tried and tested in the laboratory of true life. They are illuminated and animated by the fruits, experiences, and insights we have received since God so gloriously visited us on Father's Day more than 21 months ago.

My friend, God is no respecter of persons. If the prophecy delivered by Dr. David Yonggi Cho years before it came to pass is correct, this revival, which he correctly placed as beginning at Pensacola, Florida, will sweep up the East Coast and across the United States to the West Coast, and America will see an outpouring of God that exceeds any we have previously seen. I am convinced that you, and every believer who longs for *more* of God, has a part to play in this great awakening from God.

I have to tell you up front that revival comes only from God. It is not the product of some program, system, or formula. Even prayer and fasting can only prepare the soil. The Lord of the harvest alone decides when and how He will come. Still we know that He loves to meet with those who seek Him early. This book simply describes how we sought Him and the lessons we learned about prayer in return. May God richly bless you with the fullness of His Holy Spirit as you pursue Him with all your heart, soul, mind, and strength. Be encouraged! I believe that revival is coming your way soon!

Chapter 1

Devilish Dominion Under Brassy Skies

I remember reading about a church where the power of God flowed in a wonderful stream of glory. The people enjoyed rich worship full of exuberance and joy. When they said, "Praise the Lord!" they meant it with all their hearts. Their words didn't resonate a bit like the "sounding brass and tinkling cymbals"[1] we hear so much in Christian circles today.

They sang songs with meaning, and the Spirit of God moved so powerfully during the song services that people often got up on their own without an altar call and walked to the altar to pray. When the old silver-haired pastor finally stood to preach, no one noticed that his voice was almost gone from years of heartfelt, Spirit-inspired preaching. He preached with depth and a rich sense of the grace of God, strengthened by the certainty that there were intercessors and prayer warriors praying for him and for those in need.

These praying men and women knew how to touch God. They had spent much of the week secreted away in prayer closets or bedrooms, praying and interceding, "O God, when our pastor stands to minister, let the anointing be on him! Let Your power be there to draw people to You." They weren't interested in being elevated above others. Neither did they want to be seen or heard by appreciative audiences. Their greatest joy, and the source of their fulfillment, came when they got alone with God and prayed fervently until God saved souls.

When the old pastor decided to retire, the history of the church was forever changed. Little did the people understand that not only was the ministry of their beloved pastor ending, but the vitality of the church was also coming to an end. Over the years they had known the depths of the rich anointing and outpouring of the Holy Ghost. Solid Bible preaching and godly leadership had embedded a strong foundation in *most* members of the congregation, drawing them ever closer to their Lord and His will.

Unfortunately, this was not true for *all* members of the congregation. The individuals on the pulpit committee felt that certain changes needed to be made. When they began their search for a new pastor, they all agreed to look for a very young man. They also agreed that it was time to do away with some of the emotionalism in worship, especially the groaning and travailing of the intercessors. The committee had no difficulty finding a preacher who met their qualifications. Sadly, they never bothered to ask God what *His* qualifications might be.

Carnal Leadership Brings Heavens of Brass
The candidate chosen by this pulpit committee perfectly matched their list of qualifications. When he preached, there was little of the irritating emotionalism they had so wanted to avoid, and the congregation seemed amazingly docile. The committee found the peace quite refreshing. One irritation did remain, however. The former pastor's most faithful (and elderly) intercessor continued to rise from her pew at the end of the service and kneel down on the carpet at the same two worn spots where her fragile knees had knelt for so many decades to plead for the souls of the lost.

The new pastor was quite uncomfortable with the intercession of this elderly saint. Indeed the altar call, when this godly woman began to intercede before God and publicly travail—"My God, send us revival. My God, give us souls this morning. Don't let souls leave here and go to hell!"—was the most difficult part of his duties. So disturbed was the new pastor that he was strongly considering discarding this politically incorrect and somewhat primitive religious ritual from the order of service. He felt that there was something spooky about it all. The former pastor, on the other hand, had looked forward to this dear saint's prayer, knowing that it poured from the heart of God. It was the Spirit of God praying and travailing through this godly woman. Unfortunately, no one in Bible college had ever covered these subjects with the new pastor of the church.

The young pastor endured this public spectacle for almost six months, but one Sunday morning after he had finished his sermon, he took action. As usual, the dear old sister was down on her knees, travailing. So lost was she in intercession that she didn't even realize that the pastor had ended his sermon without giving an altar call. "Oh God, oh God," she cried, her little wrinkled face wet with tears.

The young pastor tapped the elderly intercessor on the shoulder and said, "Honey, there won't be any more need for that. We don't want that in this church because it hinders newcomers from coming. They just don't understand it." The pastor didn't know it, but by his ignorant actions that day, he posted an ancient Hebrew name *Ichabod* over the front door of the church. This means "the glory of the Lord has departed."[2]

Where Is the Touch of God?

Today you can go into any average church and hear a man preach with great oratorical ability. You can hear the resonance of his trained voice and observe his noble posture. You might notice his immaculate, custom-tailored dress suit and enjoy the fine singing of the choir. You will also most certainly see expensive equipment and a beautifully decorated sanctuary. You may even perceive a certain attentiveness in the congregation. *But where, oh where, is the touch of God?*

America's churches compete with one another to draw the rich and the famous and to fill their pews with the elite movers and shakers of their cities. Nearly every upscale neighborhood is dotted with new, user-friendly church buildings that are carefully designed to appeal to and draw the highest numbers of socially acceptable attendees. Still the rolls of the Church continue to drop and the moral climate of our nation has virtually hit bottom. Christians are barely distinguishable from non-Christians, and the Church and her leaders are held in the highest contempt. In truth, our eyes are on ourselves while God's eyes are on the many souls that hang in the balance. Something is terribly wrong. Unless somebody rediscovers how to touch God, and unless somebody is willing to pay the high price of revival, true revival will only be something we remember from bygone days.

God never puts revival on sale. He never discounts it. It always costs the same for every generation.

Prayer is in disfavor across the land. Some say, "It just doesn't work." Others say, "It requires too much effort." Yet there are many sincere people who are frustrated because their prayers are not answered. They even repeat a biblical phrase when they tell me, "When I pray, it almost seems like the heavens are brass. I just don't know what's wrong." My friend, after years of prayer and searching, I have discovered that "heavens of brass" perfectly describes the crisis of the Church in this hour! Breaking through heavens of brass is the key to revival.

Disobedience Causes Brassy Heavens

The Church is losing the battle for men's souls. Many Christians will quickly admit that they spend most of their days living in virtual defeat, almost as if they live under a cloud all the time. The truth is that they do! We have overlooked the fact that the Bible describes echelons or hierarchies of powers, rulers, and evil principalities in the heavens that impede the progress of the Church on the earth. Our disobedience increases this demonic power over us. To help us understand this more easily, let's look at some of the blessings and curses that God declared to physical Israel (the nation) and spiritual Israel (the Church) in the Book of Deuteronomy.

The Blessing

And all these blessings shall come on thee, and overtake thee, if thou shalt hearken unto the voice of the Lord thy God. Blessed shalt thou be in the city, and blessed shalt thou be in the field (Deuteronomy 28:2-3).

The Curse

*But it shall come to pass, if thou wilt not hearken unto the voice of the Lord thy God... And **thy heaven that is over thy head shall be brass, and the earth that is under thee shall be iron*** (Deuteronomy 28:15,23).

We have forgotten that hordes of demonic spirit-beings led by satan are doing everything in their power to pull us down to their level of diabolical depravity. The apostle Paul made it clear that most of his battles were against *spiritual* foes.[3] Demonic powers were the real force motivating, guiding, and empowering the men and institutions that hindered the work of God in the first century. This is still true today, but we don't realize it because the Church, by and large, has abandoned the ways of the Spirit in favor of the traditions of men. It is no accident that we are continually defeated in every area of our lives—our marriages, our homes, our churches, and our nations.

Most Christian work is done in the physical or natural realm because we think and act like we are dealing with mere mortal men. We exploit every new method we can dream up to turn our churches into a "home and garden" religion. We want everything to be nice and tidy. We don't want any discomfort or confrontation, so we carefully avoid the conviction of sin. We put on stage productions. We call in the latest and greatest evangelists. We buy all kinds of media time to broadcast our services. But seldom do we think about dealing with the *strongman* who rules so many lives and communities! Unless these demonic forces are understood and dealt with, they will certainly hinder the move of God's Spirit.

We are blind to the problem in the heavens because we are focused on the "seen" instead of the "unseen." We work through men to reach men, instead of asking the Spirit of God to move on men's hearts to bring them to their knees.

What would happen if we abandoned our useless man-made methods to reach the lost? What would happen if we cried out in the name of Jesus, who alone has the power and authority to disarm principalities and rulers of darkness? My friend, this is an important key for breaking through brass heavens. When we turn from the ways of man and cling to the power of God, we will see men's hearts changed, their bodies healed, and their lives mended.

Over the last decade, I have learned that God is sick and tired of seeing us do things our way. He is weary of hearing us blame Him for not blessing our mess. We have no right to gripe when we insist on regulating our efforts to reach men and stubbornly lean on our man-made methodologies rather than on the raw power of fervent prayer. If we want genuine revival, we will have to do things God's way. Period.

God has life fixed so that it won't work without Him.

He warned us that if we fail to do things His way, "...thy [your] heaven that is over thy [your] head shall be brass...."[4] What "heaven" is God talking about, and how can it be brass?

Let's look closely at this verse. God was talking about *your* heaven that is over *your* head. Heaven can be open to you without being open to the one standing beside you. Jesus expressed this principle in Matthew 24:40:

Then shall two be in the field; the one shall be taken, and the other left.
Heaven was open over one person in the field, but closed over the other.

Many years ago one of the most popular comic strips was called "Pogo." One of the characters in this strip always had a black cloud hovering above him. No matter where he went or what he did, he had his own personal black cloud just over his head. This may be one of the most accurate portrayals of brassy heavens that we will ever see. If we believe the lies of the devil, we are putting our futures, our families, and our churches into his hands and allowing him to shut the heavens over our heads. Paul warned us not to give place to the devil.[5]

Sin Makes the Heavens Brass

Here in the southern United States, we say that sour milk has "clabbered" once curds appear, since it has thickened and grown cloudy. Sin does the same to the heavens. Sin thickens the heavens so that they eventually become hardened to our prayers, like brass is hardened and made resistant to fire and pressure. Sin separates us from the purity and openness of God's provision.

The Bible says,

In the beginning God created the heaven and the earth (Genesis 1:1).

The heavens were clean. There was no spiritual pollution, no hierarchy or echelons of demons, powers, principalities, or dark rulers in the heavens affecting the earth. God looked at the twinkling stars, the planets, and the vast expanse of the heavens He had made, and pronounced them good.

Later Adam sinned, relinquishing his God-given authority to the devil. That gave satan a new title in his function as the leaseholder and chief governing authority of this fallen planet. Paul told the Ephesians,

*...in time past ye walked according to the course of this world, according to the **prince of the power of the air**, the spirit that now worketh in the **children of disobedience*** (Ephesians 2:2).

In the beginning, God spoke with His creation without hindrance. The sin of Adam brought separation and limited communication between God and man. Each generation wandered further from God until only Noah continued to recognize the voice of his Maker. A whole generation was shut out from the ark and from God. After the Great Flood, Noah's descendants quickly forgot God's voice, so God began to search for a man He could talk to. He found Abram. Through Abram's faith, God once again gained entrance into the affairs of men. Covenant was established, and even to this day, nearly 4,000 years later, God still passes the blessings of Abraham down to us.[6]

Our ability to receive these blessings is significantly impaired by our sin because sin impedes our prayers and prevents us from hearing the voice of God's Spirit deep in our hearts. It gives satan the authority to come in and rule over us. The devil cannot do anything unless we give him the power. Persistent, willful sin—the choice to do what we want to do—gives the devil that power. Adam legally mortgaged this world system to the devil through sin. He bartered man's divine birthright for a taste of satan's evil.

Satan immediately went to work like he was playing a cosmic game of "Monopoly." Quickly he developed a sinister master plan, assessing where and how he would establish strongholds, and what he would use to lure God's fallen creatures into his territory. His obvious objective was to accumulate as much as possible, as quickly as possible. No tactic was absent from his arsenal of weapons. Deception, lies, dulled minds—these were but a few of the traps he used to entice men into his kingdom.

Some human institutions yielded quickly to his influence, giving satan the opportunity to amass significant wealth and authority. Others have been slower to yield control into his hand. They have more successfully resisted his demands. Still, even in these places on the fringes of the devil's kingdom, his power and influence are consistently felt.

But redeemed saints are regaining control of what the devil has taken. They are confessing their sin and obeying God's Word. Land that was once under the dominion of satan is becoming holy ground. Although these holy places have been disappearing for years, the revival of God's presence in the earth will once again bring them back.

Historically, the Church has squandered her strength. She has given in to distractions and infighting. She has been lured by this world's riches and dulled by impotent religion. She has given the devil every opportunity to consolidate his power over the nations.

Years before revival arrived in Brownsville, I felt that satan was trying to establish a strong principality over the Pensacola area. I sensed satanism, witchcraft, greed, and sexual lusts settling over the area for an extended siege. It is clear that satan is trying to firmly set powerful principalities over other cities and localities as well.

I encountered such evil dominion one day when my wife, Brenda, and I were en route to San Bernardino, California, from Phoenix, Arizona. Crossing the desert, just before entering the San Bernardino area, I felt my spirit suddenly begin to shrivel and shrink as an awful heaviness tried to settle down on me. Brenda also felt the oppression.

Later on we invited a friend from San Jose, California, to preach at the church we were pastoring at that time. During a casual conversation, this man said, "You know, John, San Bernardino is one of the strongest centers of witchcraft in the nation—as a matter of fact, in the world!" He had my undivided attention. I could still remember the oppression I had felt that dark night in the desert outside of San Bernardino. He said, "There are more ritualistic sacrifices conducted in that desert area than in any other place in the nation." My spirit had picked up the presence and evil influence of a demonic strongman hovering over that region and city.

I have sensed the same kind of oppression in many key cities across America, especially in the city of New Orleans. Some of the most powerful men of God in our day, whom we love, have "met their Waterloo" under the powerful influence of the lustful strongman seated over that city. Is everyone in New Orleans dominated by evil spirits? *Absolutely not!* I have many personal friends who are strong Christians and ministers there. However, wherever an evil strongman is seated in authority over a city, Christians and churches encounter greater resistance, and it becomes more difficult to win the lost, because of the extreme power wielded by the hellish influence overhead.

At times I have felt helpless as I have seen how successfully the devil is entangling the Church. He leads her astray with grand distractions and diversions. He turns her attention from worshiping God to things that are not God's. For example, some have made an idol of their one-time salvation experience, worshiping it in place of the God of their salvation. We act like once we have our ticket to Heaven, we can do anything we want, in any way we think is right. We have become content to casually worship a God we hardly know. We have forgotten His Word and no longer seek Him in the cool of the evening. We go our own way and expect Him to meet us there, but He cannot and will not bless sin, selfishness, or rebellion! As long as there is sin in our lives, the heavens will remain brass over our heads, and satan will increase the territory under his dominion. Only prayer, coupled with obedience, can stop his desperate bid for power.

The skies were brassy when Jesus was born to a virgin. Prayer and obedience were His keys to break through the brass and hear His Father's voice. Because sin and religious tradition ruled the day, mankind had to be content to hear from God only through angels or personal visitation. All that was about to change. Our Lord's obedience to His Father's will, and His powerful intercession, blasted a hole in the brass that blocked Heaven.

> *Who in the days of His flesh, when He had offered up prayers and supplications with strong crying and tears unto Him that was able to save Him from death, and was heard in that He feared; though He were a Son,* **yet learned He obedience** *by the things which He suffered; and being made perfect, He became the author of eternal salvation unto all them that* **obey** *Him* (Hebrews 5:7-9).

The Absence of Prayer Produces Brassy Heavens

Today we are at a disadvantage. There are not as many Christians bombarding Heaven as those faithful saints of days gone by used to do. This nation has become so self-centered and pleasure-minded that we have neglected to pray. We are so distracted caring for our own affairs that we are failing to seek the face of God. The heavens have hardened. Our prayers go unanswered and the power of God is no longer evident in the earth.

In 1989, the Lord spoke to my heart and said, "Son, warn the Church to pray. Tell My people to start praying, for the heavens that were once clear are now becoming brass." That warning is as urgent today as it was then. My friend, we must pray. We must pray under the anointing and with great courage. We must boldly confront demonic principalities and strongholds. Our names should cause demonic knees to shake because of our determination to pray.

Those who persevere in their pursuit of God will be victorious. These folks will be known in hell, as were the first apostles. Peter the fisherman persevered through his failures and shortcomings. He persevered through the pain of the guilt of betraying his Lord. He endured the Lord's loving correction after His resurrection. Later he became Peter the apostle, who exercised total authority over demons in Jesus' name. When others who had not paid the price of submission and total dedication to Christ tried to exercise authority over demons like Peter had done, they discovered that they were not known in hell.

> *Then certain of the vagabond Jews, exorcists, took upon them to call over them which had evil spirits the name of the Lord Jesus, saying, We adjure you by Jesus whom Paul preacheth. And there were seven sons of one Sceva, a Jew, and chief of the priests, which did so. And the evil spirit answered and said, **Jesus I know, and Paul I know; but who are ye?** And the man in whom the evil spirit was leaped on them, and overcame them, and prevailed against them, so that they fled out of that house naked and wounded. And this was known to all the Jews and Greeks also dwelling at Ephesus; and fear fell on them all, and the name of the Lord Jesus was magnified* (Acts 19:13-17).

Remove the Obstacles to Revival

As we entered the 1990's, I realized how desperately I wanted more of God. I ached to see the lost saved, but I felt powerless and ineffective. I felt like our congregation was powerless too, even though we had been praying on a regular basis. This sense of powerlessness changes only when we resolve to remove the obstacles to revival that make the heavens brass over our heads.

I used to pastor a church in a rural area where one elderly farmer in my church had a three-acre fishing pond on his property. One day the water supply that fed into the pond became clogged and the water stopped flowing. Within a short time, all the teeming amphibious life in that pond died from suffocation and the algae took over. After a while that beautiful little fishing pond was reduced to a stinking cesspool. When the farmer unclogged the source of fresh water, the life-giving flow was restored and life eventually returned to that pond.

Our lives are like that stagnant pond. We are denied the life-giving presence and power of God because we have allowed our carnal leadership at home and in the church, our disobedience, our sin, and our lack of prayer to clog our fellowship with our Source. Remember, the devil only exercises authority when it is given to him. Only repentance and an unrelenting pursuit of God will break his power and rescue our cities and nations from his dominion.

I don't know how much of a stronghold the devil has on America, but I can tell you that God isn't finished with this nation. I sense a fracturing taking place. Breakthrough is beginning! God dearly loves the people of this nation, and He is sounding a wakeup call to our churches! He has already paid the price for our freedom. Now He is asking us, "Will you pay the price to save your land?"

Bow Your Knee

The Word says,

Submit *yourselves therefore to God.* **Resist** *the devil, and he will* **flee** *from you* (James 4:7).

Our problem is that we conveniently forget the first half of that verse! We like the "fleeing" part, but we avoid the "submitting" part like the plague. The truth is that no fleeing will take place until the submitting takes place. If the devil isn't fleeing from you, don't blame God. If you want the enemy to flee, you have to yield. You must submit to God.

If we fail to bow our knees before God, the heavens over our heads will remain brass. This will be evident everywhere. There will be few conversions to Christ. We will not see hungry people being baptized in the Holy Ghost. True revival will not come.

My friend, *we cannot afford not to have true revival*! I don't know about you, but I have seen so much painted fire (an imitation of true revival), and I have seen so much smoke from work born in man's head instead of God's heart, that I am absolutely sick! We hear people talk about revival, but many times we discover that their "rain clouds" have not rained a drop. Oh, there was some thunder and flashes of lightning, but true revival was nowhere to be found. Those clouds never gave rain! People left out after the show are as dry as ever—there was no change and they are disillusioned once again. No wonder people are hesitant to believe. No wonder they immediately conclude that it's just another cloud with no rain.

What Does the Church Really Need?

I don't believe that the greatest need of the church is another sermon. We hear sermons all the time. Neither do we need to hear or sing a new worship song. Both are good and necessary, but what we desperately need is the discipline of obeying God and His Word. Obedience opens; disobedience shuts! We need to lay down our lives in prayer and help raise up others who will join us as we seek God's face, not just His hand.

If our heavens have become brass, we need to examine ourselves and say, "Have we disobeyed God and neglected to pray?" The *first thing* Jesus did when He entered into His adult ministry at the age of 30 was to go away alone to a desert place, where He prayed and fasted!

Listen, my friend: If the very Son of God felt the need to pray to the Father so fervently and unceasingly before He ministered, how can you and I justify our prayerless ways? We can't. No explanation will do. We need obedient and powerful prayer warriors who will bombard satan's domain, rocking his evil principalities and rulers of darkness with gate-destroying prayers to God and bold declarations of His Word. We need to blast a hole in the heavens so the blessings of God can again come down.

We have seen fervent prayer and determined obedience blast holes in heavens of brass over Pensacola and other places in the United States and around the world. We have seen the glory of God come suddenly under clear heavens and envelop thousands of worshipers in His weighty presence! Believe me, once you taste and see just how good the Lord's presence can be, you will never settle for second-best blessings under cloudy heavens of brass. Revival is here, but if you want it to come to you, your city, and your church, you must battle the enemy until an opening appears in the heavens of brass! Get serious. It is time to see God's glory descend upon you in all His incredible power and beauty. The world is waiting for the Church to get right with God—*submitting to Him* and resisting the devil *with great warfare.*

Endnotes

1. See 1 Corinthians 13:1.
2. See 1 Samuel 4:21.
3. See Ephesians 6:12.
4. Deuteronomy 28:23.
5. See Ephesians 4:27.
6. See Galatians 3:7-9,14; 4:28.

Chapter 2

The Devil Traffics in Dry Places

According to your holiness, so shall be your success.
A holy man is an awesome weapon in the hands of God.
Robert Murray M'Cheyne (1813-1843)

The scene was chaotic when I drove up to the row of old Quonset huts on the Warner Robins Air Force Base in Georgia, where I pastored at the time. I had been asked to speak to a small group of workers on the base that day, but I remember the dogs most clearly. Several military police officers were trying to restrain some German shepherds that looked like they had gone mad. They were barking wildly, growling, and straining with every muscle in their bodies to lunge toward a car that was parked near the officers. Then the senior officer looked toward the dogs and suddenly shouted out with a voice of command, "Heel!"

Instantly those agitated dogs sat down on their haunches, and the restraining leashes went slack. The dogs were still quivering—with their ears erect, their eyes wide with excitement, and their mouths salivating in their eagerness to go—but they no longer jumped and pulled wildly.

As I witnessed this amazing change, I realized that I was watching a canine drug detection unit going through a training exercise. These were highly trained drug-sniffing dogs that smelled the drugs the MPs had planted in the parked car. This was what made them so agitated. Nevertheless, this wasn't the point of the training exercise. The MPs already knew that the dogs could smell the drugs, since they had been created with that natural ability. The training exercise had been designed to test their obedience, and the dogs had passed the test.

Obedience Is of Utmost Importance to God

Obedience means more to God than any set of gifts, abilities, or accomplishments. Compare Samson and Joseph for a moment. Both rose from obscurity to become deliverers of Israel. One used the supernatural strength in his body to rescue God's people; the other triumphed by depending completely on God.

Samson and Joseph were also alike in that each faced sexual temptation at a crucial point in his life. Samson's life was put on the line when he was enticed by Delilah's flattering attention. Ignoring the direct command of God not to marry, and definitely not to fornicate with, women who served other gods, Samson panted after Delilah and strained against God's command. In the end he pursued his own lusts, using God's supernatural strength to do so.

Joseph, in his time of temptation, completely resisted both his own youthful lusts and the advances of Potiphar's lustful wife. Listening to the command of God, he immediately fled from this woman's grasp. In essence, Joseph "heeled" at God's command. He passed the test of obedience and was rewarded with a long life filled with God's provision and blessings. The purpose for which he had been born was safeguarded and released by his obedience.

Samson, on the other hand, failed his test of obedience and suffered greatly at the hands of his enemies. Cruel treatment, blindness, and humiliation were Samson's lot as his enemies publicly mocked him, using the gift of strength God had given him. In the end, Samson redeemed himself and fulfilled his mission only by sacrificing his own life.

The lives of King Saul and King David also show the truth that obedience is of utmost importance to God. Saul was born with all the natural attributes of a king. By birth, he was a leader with a charismatic personality and countenance. Still, the river of God's glory did not flow in his life as it did in David's because Saul, like Samson, failed the test of obedience. He cared more for the praise of men than for the approval of God. Therefore his life has become one of the Bible's most powerful symbols of rebellion against God. Nearly every Christian can quote the words Samuel spoke to Saul because of his disobedience.

...Behold, to obey is better than sacrifice, and to hearken than the fat of rams. For rebellion is as the sin of witchcraft, and stubbornness is as iniquity and idolatry... (1 Samuel 15:22-23).

Thus there were two kings in the same room. King David carried the anointing under an open heaven to rule Israel. King Saul forfeited his anointing under a heaven of brass. King David ministered to Saul on the harp from the anointing that flowed from an open sky. King Saul, on the other hand, desperately sought relief from his demons with no help from a clabbered sky. Saul's disobedience utterly closed the heavens over his head and drove him to a witch for counsel, eventually leading him to suicide and the destruction of his family line.

Some people may say, "Well, Pastor, that was then and this is now." They have forgotten that God doesn't change. He still hates iniquity and rebellion. In fact, the two things God talks about the most in the Bible are obedience and disobedience. No matter how fast we talk, we will never be able to divert the Lord from this subject. Jesus was direct and blunt about His opinion of our excuses, justifications, and explanations for disobedience.

Many will say to Me in that day, Lord, Lord, have we not prophesied in Thy name? and in Thy name have cast out devils? and in Thy name done many wonderful works? And then will I profess unto them, I never knew you: depart from Me, ye that work iniquity. ... And every one that heareth these sayings of Mine, and doeth them not, shall be likened unto a foolish man, which built his house upon the sand (Matthew 7:22-23,26).

Make no mistake about it: *The river of God will not flow in a bed of disobedience.* Sin causes the abundant river of the Spirit to dry up in our lives. It produces spiritual and natural drought and puts us in a very dangerous position.

Jesus was born under thickened skies that had resisted the word of God for 400 long years. No prophet or preacher had spoken anointed words from Heaven for four centuries. By the time Jesus was born, the sin of rebellion had produced dry religion, captivity, poverty, widespread disease, and unchecked demonic activity in the earth.

You Will See Open Heavens

Before the cross and the advent of the Holy Spirit on the earth, the atmosphere on this planet was so permeated with evil that no one alive today could even begin to imagine what life was like under this stifling blanket. Solomon described the nightmare of life under thickened skies:

> *So I returned, and considered all the oppressions that are done under the sun: and* [I beheld] *the tears of such as were oppressed, and they had no comforter; and* **on the side of their oppressors there was power; but they had no comforter** (Ecclesiastes 4:1).

Solomon was prophetically looking forward to the cross. Things were so bad during his lifetime that it was better that men not even be born! As bad as things may appear to be right now, our world is wonderful compared to Solomon's world. Notice that Solomon complained that the people had "no comforter" and "no power."

God's Son, armed with a secret He could hardly wait to reveal to His oppressed followers, stepped right into the middle of this depressing picture of darkness, ignorance, and hopelessness. He knew that the world was about to change forever—a change He promised during His earthly ministry when He said that God would send His people a *Comforter*, and they would receive *power!*[1] With the coming of God's Spirit, men and women no longer need to live oppressed, suppressed, and depressed, such as they did during Solomon's lifetime.

> *Jesus saw Nathanael coming to Him, and saith of him, Behold an Israelite indeed, in whom is no guile! Nathanael saith unto Him, Whence knowest Thou me? Jesus answered and said unto him, Before that Philip called thee, when thou wast under the fig tree, I saw thee. Nathanael answered and saith unto Him, Rabbi, Thou art the Son of God; Thou art the King of Israel. Jesus answered and said unto him,*

*Because I said unto thee, I saw thee under the fig tree, believest thou? thou shalt see greater things than these. And He saith unto him, Verily, verily, I say unto you, Hereafter ye **shall see heaven open**, and the angels of God ascending and descending upon the Son of man* (John 1:47-51).

Jesus was telling Nathanael that he was going to see what happens when the heavens open and the Spirit of God becomes active in our world. Nathanael would literally see the manifestations of ministering spirits working in tandem with the Son of God. Did Jesus mean that the clouds would roll back miraculously and a wide staircase would suddenly appear with angels skipping up and down the steps? Certainly not.

On a clear day when the sky is bright blue, even a casual glance will tell you there is nothing between you and space. Even when the skies are overcast, the clouds have no power to separate you from the Lord. Jesus was referring to a heaven that is not rooted in the natural realm. This heaven does not respond to the earthly laws of physics. Jesus was talking about the same skies or heavens that can become brass through the disobedience of mankind.

Jesus wasn't interested in becoming the main attraction of a big Bible conference. He didn't seek popularity. He didn't expect the title of "Rabboni," or "great teacher." He wanted to touch us right where we live. He wanted to obey His Father, and He wanted to see His disciples follow in His footsteps. When Jesus told Nathanael that he would see Heaven open, He was saying that Nathanael would be an eyewitness to the Lord's victorious life of obedience, even under hopelessly thickened clouds of brass. He was saying that Nathanael would see the fruit of total obedience.

Jesus was fully God and fully man, but He didn't draw on His deity to overcome the world, the flesh, or the devil. He overcame it all as an anointed *man* because He knew that was how *you and I* would have to overcome our obstacles. Otherwise it would have been totally unfair for Him to say, "Follow Me."[2] He could have shown His omnipotence, omniscience, and omnipresence on earth because He was, after all, the only begotten Son of God. Instead He chose not to move in these divine powers so that He could legally invade the realm of the flesh as a man. Referring to Himself as the Son of man, He pointedly emphasized His birth through the obedience of a very human mother and showed us how to live as a man who perfectly obeyed His Father.

1. *Jesus did not move in omnipotence on earth.* He was obedient and dependent.

    > *The Son can do nothing of Himself, but what He seeth the Father do: for what things soever He doeth, these also doeth the Son likewise* (John 5:19b).

2. *Jesus did not move in omniscience on earth.* He told His disciples concerning His second coming,

    > *But of that day and that hour knoweth no man, no, not the angels which are in heaven, **neither the Son**, but the Father* (Mark 13:32).

    What He learned, He discovered the old-fashioned way—through prayer, through study of the Scriptures, and through long hours in communion with God the Father. Had Jesus been omniscient, He would have known when He was coming back.

3. *Jesus was not omnipresent on earth.*

    > *Then said Martha unto Jesus, Lord, if Thou hadst been here, my brother had not died* (John 11:21).

    Jesus could be in only one place at a time because He was not omnipresent. This is why He said,

    > *...It is expedient for you that I go away...* (John 16:7).

God is always interested in the fruit of our lives—the fruit of obedience. Nearly every book in the Bible speaks of the effects of God's presence in the lives of men and women. The parable of the talents is about fruits.[3] Likewise, the Book of Revelation is about fruits. Every time Jesus spoke to one of the seven churches through the prophecy of John, He commended them for their godly fruit or chastised them for their lack of fruit. Using the phrase "to him that overcome," Jesus showed every one of the churches the benefits of obedience and perseverence.

Ephesus

To him that overcometh will I give to eat of the tree of life, which is in the midst of the paradise of God (Revelation 2:7b).

Smyrna
He that overcometh shall not be hurt of the second death (Revelation 2:11b).

Pergamos
To him that overcometh will I give to eat of the hidden manna, and will give him a white stone, and in the stone a new name written, which no man knoweth saving he that receiveth it (Revelation 2:17b).

Thyatira
And he that overcometh, and keepeth My works unto the end, to him will I give power over the nations: and he shall rule them with a rod of iron; as the vessels of a potter shall they be broken to shivers: even as I received of My Father. And I will give him the morning star (Revelation 2:26-28).

Sardis
He that overcometh, the same shall be clothed in white raiment; and I will not blot out his name out of the book of life, but I will confess his name before My Father, and before His angels (Revelation 3:5).

Philadelphia
Him that overcometh will I make a pillar in the temple of My God, and he shall go no more out: and I will write upon him the name of My God, and the name of the city of My God, which is new Jerusalem, which cometh down out of heaven from My God: and I will write upon him My new name (Revelation 3:12).

Laodicea
To him that overcometh will I grant to sit with Me in My throne, even as I also overcame, and am set down with My Father in His throne (Revelation 3:21).

God has never lifted His requirement that we overcome sin and the devil. If Jesus told every church in the Book of Revelation to overcome, I think it is important to God that you and I overcome as well! To each of us He says, "To him that overcometh..." not "To him who muddles his way through in failure, selfishness, and foolishness...."

Obedience Opens the Heavens
The fruit of obedience was, and still is, the privilege of seeing the heavens overhead open. Obedience to God always produces a

supernatural flow of His anointing. This ministry from God's throne ensures that His will is done on earth as in Heaven.

Nathanael walked, talked, and shared meals and ministry with Jesus for more than three years. With his own eyes, he watched the Master put the devil to flight. He saw fear banished, blind eyes opened, and the lame walking. He saw lifelong captives forever freed from demon possession, physical affliction, and spiritual oppression.

Today we have the living Spirit of God dwelling within us. We have the wealth of God's Word, as well as the knowledge and ability to read the Scriptures for ourselves. We have the name of Jesus and the authority of His shed blood in our arsenal of lethal spiritual weapons.

Walk in the Miraculous!

Don't get religious and stick these things into some "nice Bible story" category. God will come through every time you obey Him, just like He did for Jesus Christ. That is the whole point of the Lord's promise to Nathanael. If you walk like Jesus walked—and remember, He did it all as a *man* who did not pull from any source other than those that are available to man—you too will see Heaven open over your life! This is true no matter how thick the heavens over your city or region may be. Jesus never meant for the miraculous life to be limited only to Himself. He ordained that you and I should walk in the miraculous too! He was the prototype of many who were to come after Him, the firstborn of many sons.

> And these signs shall follow them that believe; In My name shall they cast out devils; they shall speak with new tongues; they shall take up serpents; and if they drink any deadly thing, it shall not hurt them; they shall lay hands on the sick, and they shall recover (Mark 16:17-18).

Satan Traffics in Dry Places

Disobedience does more than cause the skies to thicken over our heads. According to God's warning in the Book of Deuteronomy, disobedience also causes the earth under our feet to become iron.[4] Iron equates to dryness, drought, and famine. It is in this arid land that the devil begins to roam.

When the unclean spirit is gone out of a man, he walketh through dry places, seeking rest, and findeth none (Matthew 12:43).

The evil one traffics in dry places because he cannot co-exist with the manifest presence of the river of God. Any area of our personal or corporate lives that lacks the life-giving flow of God's Spirit is ripe for occupation by our most spiteful enemy.

The sin of disobedience robs us of the ability to prosper, and steals our health. It brings pain to our path and bruises our feet with cruel, cold hardness. It produces thick darkness and cuts off our productivity, our prosperity, and our very means of survival. It breeds guilt and makes us difficult to live with because it separates us from God and puts a wedge between us and other believers.

Think about the times you have disobeyed God. I am sure that no one had to tell you when the heavens over your head were hardening. You knew that something had come between you and your Lord! Whenever you do not repent and remove the sin that separates you from God, the heavens become brass and you eventually *suffer*. Your family suffers, your friends suffer, and even your church suffers. Long before the clouds begin to gather over your head, the Spirit within gives you a clear sense that things are not right. You know it, your wife knows it, your children know it, and even the unsaved people around you know it. But the plain truth is that none of them can do anything about it. Repentance is a job that you alone can do.

God said through the Psalmist that the one who keeps His Word "...shall be like a tree planted by the rivers of water, that bringeth forth his fruit in his season; his leaf also shall not wither; and whatsoever he doeth shall prosper."[5] This means that even if a drought strikes where you live, you will prosper if you are planted by the river of God!

The devil is powerless when you walk in unbroken fellowship with the Lord. He may have the *ability* to do evil, but he does not have the *authority*—unless you give it to him. As long as you are obedient to the call of Christ Jesus, the minions of hell will see you as someone who is known in hell! Keep yourself strong in the Spirit by feeding on God's Word, by meditating on His precepts, and by checking the Spirit's barometric pressure over your head. True, the devil will continue to harass and buffet you, trying to hinder your every attempt to draw near to God; but he cannot harm you as long as the heavens are clear and open between you and God! Prayer coupled with obedience is the only way you can keep the heavens clear.

The Smallest Piece of the Pie

If you diagram the time spent in worship services each week in a typical congregation, prayer makes up the smallest piece of the pie. Announcements are given more time. Auxiliary activities are given more time. The receiving of tithes and offerings is given more time. Music is given more time. Preaching is given more time. The smallest slice of the pie is always given to prayer.

This is true not only for worship services, but for the activities of the church as a whole. For example, if you call a meeting for almost anything other than prayer, you will draw a crowd. A prayer meeting, on the other hand, will attract only a handful of people.

How sad! We must refocus our hearts and redirect our energies. Jesus said,

My house shall be called the house of prayer... (Matthew 21:13).

We have most certainly forgotten this. Our erroneous man-made priorities have misled us. If we are to come into God's house and pursue His desires, we will spend much more time in prayer. We will do warfare, pressing in and punching holes through the brassy heavens. Then satan will have no effect on our lives. He will hold no power over our churches. Until then we suffer the effects of his presence. The heavens over our heads become as brass.

Endnotes

1. See John 14:26; Acts 1:8.
2. See Matthew 4:19.
3. See Matthew 25:14-30.
4. See Deuteronomy 28:23.
5. Psalm 1:3.

Chapter 3

Eight Obstacles to Brass-Shattering Prayer

I heard a friend of mine say that many doctors believe we are all born with cancer cells in our body. In fact, new cancer cells continue to appear until the day we die! Why then don't we all get cancer? God endowed us with an immune system that destroys cancer cells with 100-percent efficiency and no side effects—until something weakens or compromises it. (This brother said he was grossly simplifying a very complex process, but most of us couldn't understand the detailed version anyway.)

We don't really get cancer. The prevailing medical theory is that we experience a breakdown in our natural defenses, thereby giving the cancerous cells that are already present in our bodies the opportunity to multiply! This is why the medical research community devotes so much time to the study of the human immune system. They hope to learn how to fix the broken immune systems in the many people who are battling cancer and how to stimulate our natural defense mechanisms so that cancer cells cannot take over our bodies. The human immune system is simply nature's most effective anti-cancer treatment for mankind. Nothing else comes close. Preventing this system from breaking down in the first place is the key to winning the war with cancer.

Types of Cells in Our Physical Bodies

As my friend and I talked more about the workings of the human body, he explained that at the heart of every cell is a minute strand of DNA. This is our genetic fingerprint. We all have a DNA print that is uniquely ours. It is the heart and mind of every cell in our bodies, including those in our fingernails, hair, skin, body organs, and blood. A normal, healthy human cell has a complete and unaltered DNA strand that contains all the information the cell will ever need for future development and function. Each time that cell multiplies and creates new cells, it passes on that information.

The Healthy Cell

A healthy cell consumes energy, occupies space, and performs a specific task in perfect harmony with neighboring cells. A number of cells follow specific DNA instructions to group together with other cells to perform specialized tasks. These cell groups form key organs such as the liver, the kidneys, the heart, the brain, the lungs, and the skin. Although such cells have special functions, they all contain the same central DNA code as every other cell in the individual's body.

The "Out-of-Place" Cell

Cells that are part of a second category seem to have lost their proper place in the body. These cells have the same primary DNA code as other cells, but they either missed out on the directions or just ignored them. Like healthy cells, they too consume energy and occupy space, but they don't seem to belong anywhere, and they don't perform any functions or work in the body. (If you are starting to feel uncomfortable, you are beginning to see just how closely this describes the Body of Christ.) These cells gather together in makeshift structures like moles, cysts, harmless growths (benign tumors), or other odd multiple-cell formations that don't have any particular purpose.

Most of the time these freeloaders don't cause any trouble— they're just a nuisance. If they grow too much, they begin to impede the function of the working cells and organs. Some of these cells appear to be especially sensitive to the touch and to changes in temperature or environment. If they are on the skin, they are generally prone to being bumped, scraped, scratched, and generally irritated by exposure to excess ultraviolet radiation and by constant friction from clothing and other body parts. Some may become so sensitive to stimulation or abrasion that they move into a third category of cells.

The Malignant Destroyer Cell

A third category of cells comes into existence when a DNA strand is damaged or altered. These cells start as benign cells whose DNA mutates afterward because of outside influences. This class of cell consumes energy at an elevated rate, with an excessive hunger for fuel. Sometimes it also occupies too much space, since it tends to multiply at such a wildly random and runaway rate that it constantly encroaches on nearby cells and organs.

The most dangerous aspect of these cells is that they are greedy, demanding, unscrupulous, and merciless in their constant drive to satisfy their raging hunger. These cells are *malignant*. Perhaps their most dreaded characteristic is their ability to metastasize or migrate from one part of the body to another. With what almost appears to be a peculiar and evil cunning, these cells constantly adapt and mutate so that they can cross barriers, infiltrate existing organs, build resistance to medical treatments, and consume nearby healthy cells. In general terms, these cells are bad. If left unchecked, they will ultimately consume the life of their host. This third class of cells constitutes the vast legion of related diseases we call cancer. It can strike any living cell in the human body, which explains why there are so many different types of cancer.

The Natural Reflects the Supernatural

The natural realm is a finite reflection of reality in the supernatural or spirit realm from which it receives its life. As there are three categories of cells in our physical bodies, so there are three broad classes of people in any local body of believers. Every believer is originally born into this world with the Ten Commandments indelibly stamped on his heart. He is also born with a sin nature inherited from Adam, his earthly ancestor. If left unchecked, this cancerous nature of sin threatens his existence. Rebirth through the blood of Christ, the second Adam, purifies his spiritual DNA, giving him the heart of God his Father.

The Healthy Believer

Healthy believers in Christ's Body consume the ministry energies of those assigned to feed the flock. They also perform tasks of service in perfect harmony with fellow believers. Under specific instructions from their spiritual DNA strand, some Christians will group together with other Christians for specialized functions within the Body, such as feeding the flock, ministering on the worship team, teaching children, etc. Yet all, from the pastor to the greeter, share a common spiritual DNA code that is unique to Christ; all share a link with one Head.

The "Out-of-Place" Believer

Every church also seems to have another group of believers who have good hearts but just don't seem to know their place or function in the local body. They are easy to spot because they never do any work in the church. They are primarily interested in being fed and in sitting in their usual place right up front where the choir members have to squeeze by them, or near the door where they can see and be seen by everybody who comes and goes. They are especially sensitive and resistant to change, so they are quick to complain if the sanctuary is too hot or cold, the sermon goes too long, or the preacher gets to "meddling." On the other hand, these believers are slow to share in the work of the congregation or to serve the larger community. They consume a higher level of the ministry staff's time and energies than believers who actively serve the Lord in the church or community. Given their inactivity, the members of this second class of believers are prone to talking more than most. This often transforms and moves them into a third class of churchgoers.

The Malignant, Devouring Believer

People in the third class of believers have allowed chronic unforgiveness to turn into bitterness, which has mutated their spiritual DNA. Once the heart of a believer has been reconfigured by bitterness, he finds it difficult to identify with the other members of the Body. Thus he is no longer content merely to occupy space and be fed. He becomes hungry for more—more recognition, more power, and more say in the operation of the church. He begins to use his tongue and power of influence to press his will on his neighbors and to consume those who won't move to his beat. The root of bitterness has given satan a place in his heart. His function has become destruction. To the outward eye, he is still a sheep; but to the discerning eye of the Spirit, he has become a devouring wolf. He has become a cancer and a blight, with a cunning determination to bring division and strife to the Body of Christ.

Prayer: God's Prescription for a Healthy Church Body

God designed the Body of Christ with a perfect system for dealing with unforgiveness and bitterness long before serious problems arise. Spiritual cancer sets in only when God's people fail to follow God's plan for healthy life and allow the Body's built-in defenses to fall. These failures are almost always traceable to the congregation's failure to pray and to follow God's Word. By definition, God's house is a house of prayer.[1] It is logical to say that if a church doesn't pray, it has no right to call itself God's house. One thing is certain: If a local body of Christ doesn't pray, it is inevitable that spiritual cancer is on the way.

Drink of the Spirit Daily for Total Spiritual Health

Another brief example from the natural realm will help us to better understand the role of prayer in the spiritual realm and in revival. A healthy human body can go for up to 40 days without food before serious life-threatening complications set in. As soon as the end of the first day of a fast, the individual may experience weakness, slight disorientation, headaches, and loss of energy, but he would survive. However, doctors say that the human body cannot safely go without water for more than three days. After that point, anyone who has drank no water risks permanent damage to the major organs in his body, which leads to imminent death as these organs begin to fail.

In a similar manner, the life of our spirit-man is nurtured as we feed on God's Word and drink of His Spirit. My friend, you may squeak by in your Christian life without reading and meditating on God's Word for some time, but if you try to wander through life without drinking from His Spirit in regular prayer, you risk a serious attack on the most treasured and vital parts of your life! A body that is separated from its head is a corpse! Prayer is the drink and life-sustaining breath of the believer and the Church. In its absence, death or serious impairment is near. I believe that God has brought revival to America to save her life! We are in God's intensive care unit. He has connected His Body to a massive influx of oxygen and life-giving fluids! The breath or river of God is reviving the life of the Church, but He wants us to begin drawing breath and seeking His Spirit without outside assistance!

Neglect and ignorance brought us to this place. Now we have no excuse. Fervent prayer is crucial for our survival, and we know it. Someone else also knows this. The adversary trembles every time he overhears a blood-washed saint make a commitment to pray. We may be blind to the truth, but the devil is not. He knows the real power of prayer in the life of a submitted saint. He fears the fires ignited by Spirit-led intercession. Therefore he will do almost anything to keep God's people from their knees.

The Adversary's Plan of Attack

The moment you step away from everyone else and kneel in a private place for prayer, every possible diversion, task, amusement, or offense will rise up in your mind and present itself as an emergency. The truth is that you wouldn't let any one of these things pull you away from your favorite television program or hobby, but in the prayer closet they seem to take on immense importance. My friend, keep your word. Fulfill your intentions. Push aside every hindrance to prayer that the devil drops into your thoughts when you kneel to pray.

In addition to the hindrances that the enemy concocts to stop our prayers, there are other obstacles that we carry into the prayer closet with us. They must be dealt with if we ever want to prevail in prayer and pierce the thickened skies above our heads.

Obstacle #1: Unforgiveness
Brass-shattering prayer will not flow through unforgiving hearts.

Unforgiveness, because it quickly turns into bitterness, is the first and perhaps most serious blockage to fervent, effective prayer. Jesus taught His disciples much about the relationship between unforgiveness and prayer.

> *Therefore if thou bring thy gift to the altar, and there rememberest that thy brother hath ought against thee; leave there thy gift before the altar, and go thy way; first be reconciled to thy brother, and then come and offer thy gift* (Matthew 5:23-24).

> *After this manner therefore pray ye: ... And forgive us our debts, as we forgive our debtors. ... But if ye forgive not men their trespasses, neither will your Father forgive your trespasses* (Matthew 6:9a,12,15).

> *And **when ye stand praying**, forgive, if ye have ought against any: that your Father also which is in heaven may forgive you your trespasses* (Mark 11:25).

The apostle Paul warned of another consequence of unforgiveness when he told the believers at Corinth:

> *To whom ye forgive any thing, I forgive also: for if I forgave any thing, to whom I forgave it, for your sakes forgave I it in the person of Christ; **lest satan should get an advantage of us:** for we are not ignorant of his devices* (2 Corinthians 2:10-11).

Unforgiveness Mimics Multiple Sclerosis

In further discussions with my friend, he said that unforgiveness strikes at the heart of our communications lines with God, much like multiple sclerosis attacks the human spinal cord and central nervous system. The Bible says,

Hatred stirreth up strifes: but love covereth all sins (Proverbs 10:12).

Love is the supernatural covering that protects, heals, and shields the Body of Christ from internal strife and injury. In the human body, a myelin sheath protects the countless nerves that are bundled together in the spinal cord, much like plastic or rubber insulation shields electrical wires from shorting out against other wires, metal objects, or conductive substances like water.

✶ When the Body Devours Itself

During our discussion about unforgiveness, my friend noted that researchers think the disease of multiple sclerosis somehow causes its victim's immune system to turn against the body. It begins by attacking the myelin sheath that protects the spinal cord, as if it were an unwanted intruder. Each attack leaves scars on the delicate spinal cord ("sclerosis" means "scarring"), until these assaults gradually begin to perforate this protective barrier. When the damage becomes severe, it causes the nerves in the spinal cord to short out like a telephone cable that has accidentally been severed. This hinders or destroys direct communication between the head and the body, causing weakness, partial paralysis, and other symptoms.

✶ Unforgiveness Short-Circuits Prayer

Unforgiveness strikes directly at our prayer cord, our vital link to our Redeemer. It cuts us off from God's forgiveness and authorizes satan to begin thickening the skies over our heads. It is one of the most deadly of all sins because it causes us to withdraw from a brother, bringing instant separation from God's life-giving flow. Any extremity or organ in the human body that is cut off from the life-giving flow of blood begins to atrophy and dies within an hour. Long-term separation brings death of tissues and the spreading rot of gangrene.

When we first come to repentance in Jesus Christ, we correctly acknowledge that Jesus has forgiven us from all our unrighteousness. However, where we hold unforgiveness in our hearts, especially toward people who have wronged us before we became believers, that unforgiveness becomes a weight that hinders our faith and disarms us of our power to pray with assurance and confidence. There is no offense worth the separation from God that we experience when we harbor unforgiveness.

Releasing the people who have harmed you and have inflicted unbearable pain on you will release you to progress in God's plan. It will free your faith to see your prayers catapulted heavenward every time you pray. The point to all this is that it doesn't pay to hold a grudge. Be slow to anger and quick to forgive! Unforgiveness is hazardous to your health. It is also material that thickens the heavens over *thy* [your] head. Out of all Ten Commandments, six deal with people-to-people (horizontal) communication and four with people-to-God (vertical) communication. God knew that we would have conflicts with each other. This is why He gave us more commandments concerning our horizontal relationships than our relationship with Him.

Obstacle #2: Regarding Iniquity
Iniquity destroys the power of brass-shattering prayer.

Eli the priest will be forever remembered for two reasons. First, he was used by God to train Samuel from his early years to adulthood. Samuel was destined to become one of God's greatest prophets. He would anoint Saul, Israel's first king, and David, Israel's greatest king.

Second, Eli raised two worthless sons who are among the most despised men in the entire Bible! Ultimately God brought judgment on Eli's house because he had *regarded iniquity* by looking the other way while his sons made a mockery of the temple and the sacrifices offered there to God. Although these young men were literally committing adultery with women right in the temple, Eli failed to correct and discipline them. Finally God did what Eli would not. Not only did God stop the blatant iniquity of Eli's sons, He also cut off the entire family line. Eli's wicked sons were both struck down when their sin allowed the hated Philistines to capture the ark of God, and Eli fell and broke his neck when heard this news. Thus Eli's family line came to a bitter end.[2]

The story of Eli should be a chilling warning to parents of every generation. We have no business trying to cover up or condone the sins of our children. God knows what they are doing. He also sees our failure to correct them. He cannot be hoodwinked or distracted from the real spiritual condition of our lives.

David wrote in the Psalms,

If I regard iniquity in my heart, the Lord will not hear me (Psalm 66:18).

Today we might say, "If I cherish lawlessness or sin in my heart, the Lord will not hear my prayers." King Saul cherished the praises of the people more than the approval of God. When confronted by the prophet of God, he cherished his reputation more than the truth and blamed his people for something he had done. Even after he realized that David had been chosen by God Himself to assume the throne of Israel, Saul vainly tried to kill God's man for many years.

The Hebrew word for "regard" in this verse is *ra'ah*. Among other things, it means "to gaze, to look joyfully, to enjoy or experience a thing."[3] Don't go into your prayer closet and expect to see the glory of God if you have been gazing upon and enjoying sin in the family room! Too many Christian homes today have become contaminated by sexually explicit videotapes, television programs, and situation comedies that scornfully ridicule righteous principles and godly living. Every time you feed on such TV programs and movies, you are literally regarding iniquity in your heart! Another meaning of *ra'ah* is "to spy and stare."[4] Brother, don't grab your wife's intimate clothing catalog and hide in the bathroom. You are spying on forbidden fruit when you look on a woman other than your wife and allow your mind to fantasize. Sin occurs in the mind and heart, even if your body never gets involved—which it does. Repent of any sin, renounce any return to that sin, and get back to the business of holiness.

Another way we regard iniquity involves the people we respect, honor, or look up to. (Don't act religious—I know you have your heroes too). God is far more interested in a man's inner character than in his outward appearance and performance. If you catch yourself idolizing an ungodly athlete, politician, actor, or actress with an ungodly lifestyle, you need to repent. You have regarded iniquity in your heart. Don't think I'm majoring on minors here. The Scriptures warn us,

Keep thy heart with all diligence; for out of it are the issues of life (Proverbs 4:23).

**Guard your heart and don't let iniquity
find a home in your life or affections.**

A lax attitude toward sin also amounts to regarding iniquity. James the apostle warned the Church about the dangers of friendship with the world and its effect on prayer:

Ye ask, and receive not, because ye ask amiss, that ye may consume it upon your lusts. Ye adulterers and adulteresses, know ye not that the friendship of the world is enmity with God? ***whosoever therefore will be a friend of the world is the enemy of God*** (James 4:3-4).

We also regard iniquity in our hearts when we cling to a position we know is unrighteous. Often we insist on justifying our actions or opinions at any cost because we don't want to admit we are wrong. This is pride. When pride lurks in the shadows, motivating this kind of attitude, it must be cast down. If pride could make a devil out of an angel, what might it do to you? You may think that you can get by. Think again!

When you refuse to accept the truth, you are embracing and endorsing a lie. Who gets the honor and glory for this kind of foolishness—God or the devil? Whose kingdom is built up and strengthened? Who is most pleased when you promote a lie to cling to a *cherished* position? Remember that the river of God will never flow through a bed of disobedience. Cast away the lie, release your pride, and cling to that which is good and true. Then the power of God can and will flow through you again.

Obstacle #3: Prejudice
When prejudice is truly done away with, brassy skies shatter.

One time a woman who was dying in a hospital called her pastor and asked for prayer. This godly pastor understood that the Holy Spirit distributes His supernatural gifts "severally as He wills"[5] among the members of His Body, so he asked a certain African American man in the church, whom he knew to operate powerfully in the gift of healing, to go to the hospital and pray for the desperately ill woman.

The woman's face lit up in anticipation when she saw the door to her hospital room open. She knew the pastor was sending someone from the church to pray for her healing, and she was hoping for a miracle. When the door swung open and she realized that her visitor was a black man, she instantly said, "No! You will *not* lay hands on me!" So insistent was she that the only thing the dismayed man could do was turn around and leave. The woman's condition kept getting worse, until the doctors finally moved her to the intensive care unit in hopes of somehow keeping her alive. Nothing else they had done seemed to be working.

Finally the woman realized that her end was near if God didn't intervene. She was so weak that she couldn't speak above a whisper, but she managed to raise her finger and attract a nurse's attention. When the nurse stepped closer and bent down, she heard the woman weakly whisper, "Please call my pastor again and ask him to come back. Tell him he can bring anyone he needs to bring to pray for me, including the black man. If I don't get a miracle, I'm going to die." The black brother returned to the hospital, but this time he stood at the woman's bedside, laid his hands on her, and offered a powerful prayer for her healing. God raised up the woman from her deathbed that day and made her whole.

The Holy Spirit divides the gifts among whomsoever He wills. Sometimes He gives the gift you need to someone you just can't stand. Sooner or later, my friend, you will have to go to this person if you want to receive what you need.

God our Father is determined to conform us to the image of His Son. This involves much change and transformation. Sometimes this means that we have to let go of prejudices and preferences that prevent us from allowing God to work in our lives. We have to accept His gifts from whatever messenger He sends. Likewise, we have to go to whatever steward God has chosen to safeguard the resource we need. The same is true among the nations.

We had to walk softly with South Africa, for example, even though we didn't like their ways. Why? They possess much of the gold and many of the gems of the world. In a similar manner, the Arabs possess most of the oil on this planet. God divided and distributed the wealth of the world as it pleased Him. Now He forces us to find ways to live together.

The African American man in this story possessed the gift that would bring the woman healing. God was ready to heal her at any time, but the woman was not ready to accept God's gift. Only when the doctors' prescriptions and treatments didn't work, and she was facing imminent death, was this woman willing not only to ask the Lord for healing but to accept His plan. All along God had the prescription the dying woman needed, but first He required her to release a sin that had a deathgrip on her life. The woman, however, felt justified in clinging to her racial prejudice even while she confessed Jesus Christ as her Lord. She refused to believe that God would bring her healing through hands that were a different skin color than her own. Once she yielded to the will of God, He saved her life through the gifts, faith, and anointed prayers of the same African American brother she had once rejected. The instant she released her prejudice, God released her healing. What will He require you to release before He brings revival to your life or to your church?

Most of the problems Paul the apostle encountered were rooted in racial and religious prejudice. This was also the root of almost every major problem in the early Church. In each case, prejudice threatened to divide the brethren and nullify the mystery of the gospel. While God honored the Jews, the descendants of Abraham, He was careful to include people from many other nations and races in the genealogy of the Messiah, since His plan was to bring all nations into His Kingdom under one blood, one banner, and one Savior, Jesus Christ.

Paul constantly battled against the religious prejudice of the Jews against Gentiles and all non-Jewish converts to Christ, but he struck a blow against almost every form of prejudice when he told the churches:

> *There is neither Jew nor Greek, there is neither bond nor free, there is neither male nor female: for ye are all one in Christ Jesus. And if ye be Christ's, then are ye Abraham's seed, and heirs according to the promise* (Galatians 3:28-29).

Paul leaves no room for racial prejudice, gender prejudice, or even occupational or economic prejudice! In God's presence, all men and women share one common status. We are all sinners saved by grace and grace alone. It is by God's grace that we are saved. It is by His grace that we dwell together in unity. All have common access to the presence of God through the name of Jesus, God's Son, and the power of His shed blood. If we insist on clinging to our prejudices, we are literally failing to recognize the true Body of Christ. This is an affront to God.

> *For by one Spirit are we all baptized into one body, whether we be Jews or Gentiles, whether we be bond or free; and have been all made to drink into one Spirit. For the body is not one member, but many. ... But now hath God set the members every one of them in the body, as it hath pleased him. ... And the eye cannot say unto the hand, I have no need of thee: nor again the head to the feet, I have no need of you. ... That there should be no schism in the body; but that the members should have the same care one for another* (1 Corinthians 12:13-14,18,21,25).

For many generations, numerous American churches preached and acted as if there was one gospel for the white man and another gospel for the black man. Every time Galatians chapter 3 was read in their meetings, it was followed by a resounding "but" and some dubious justification for condoning prejudice. The same drama recently took place in South Africa. In both the

United States and South Africa, people held to their opinions so stubbornly that blood was shed and thousands of people died needlessly. Obedience to God's Word would have saved both nations from the unspeakable sorrow and heartbreak they endured through civil conflict.

My friend, any time you catch yourself saying, "Yes, but..." when you are reading the Word of God, ask yourself why you are butting your head against God! Somebody is in error, and it isn't God. Prejudice inflicts misery and strife on the people of nearly every continent of the world. It has spawned countless bloody wars and conflicts. Nearly every tyrant who has risen to imprison and overpower other nations was propelled into power by the sheer force of hatred and prejudice. One mark of *true revival* is that it gathers all people under the Son, bridging the chasms that separate the races, the genders, and the many social and ethnic groups of the world.

Obstacle #4: Judgment of Others
**A heart that judges dilutes the force
of the prayers intended to break through brass.**

Judgmentalism is another sin that blocks or hinders our prayers. Jesus warned His disciples and all who would trust in Him:

Judge not, that ye be not judged. For with what judgment ye judge, ye shall be judged: and with what measure ye mete, it shall be measured to you again. And why beholdest thou the mote that is in thy brother's eye, but considerest not the beam that is in thine own eye? Or how wilt thou say to thy brother, Let me pull out the mote out of thine eye; and, behold, a beam is in thine own eye? Thou hypocrite, first cast out the beam out of thine own eye; and then shalt thou see clearly to cast out the mote out of thy brother's eye (Matthew 7:1-5).

He also told a hostile crowd of religious leaders,
Judge not according to the appearance, but judge righteous judgment (John 7:24).

You may occasionally have to judge the fruits of righteousness in a person's life, but that doesn't mean God has called you to a new career as "holy fruit inspector." This is nothing more than a fancy name for gossiping and self-righteous hypocrisy. Follow the counsel of Jesus: Judge not so you won't be judged.

We love to judge. We love to compare others to ourselves, the best example of godliness we know. We like to compare the doctrines of others to the most accurate doctrine we know—ours. We delight in judging another's children, clothing, careers, and spouses, hoping to find that they are far inferior to ours. We scrutinize one another's vacations, cars, furniture, and homes. We land powerfully self-righteous judgments on pastors, their teaching and preaching, and everything their wives try to do. All the while, we are building our apparent goodness and trying to confirm our favor with God and man. We truly have the uncanny ability to see ourselves as more gifted, better equipped, and more compassionate than almost anyone around.

Most of us know better than to outright brag. Instead, we couch our superiority in genuine-sounding concerns about the less fortunate in our churches or workplaces. "Thank God we are there to fill the gap when all these lesser life forms fail," is our attitude. This nonsense is standard operating procedure in churches all over the world. It keeps the heavens brass and prevents true intercession from arising in our hearts unto the Lord.

Administering a Spiritual Forensics Test

I wonder how many people "sleep before their time"? What would happen if we exhumed them from their graves and ran a spiritual forensics test? We might find that physical disease had nothing to do with their untimely deaths! In fact, we might discover that they died from the spiritual disease of judgmentalism and their refusal to accept those they dislike as joint members in the Body of Christ. Paul the apostle was blunt when he wrote to the Corinthians about properly observing communion.

For he that eateth and drinketh unworthily, eateth and drinketh damnation to himself, not discerning the Lord's body. For this cause many are weak and sickly among you, and many sleep. For if we would judge ourselves, we should not be judged (1 Corinthians 11:29-31).

Bitterness, unforgiveness, and prejudice can all manifest themselves as judgmentalism that wrongfully excludes people from God's Kingdom. When we judge others, we bring God's judgment on our own heads. (It is also possible that some children have cut short their lives because they failed to honor their parents in childhood and later as adults.)

The cure is simple. Let Jesus be your plumb line. This sobering appraisal will most certainly silence the hypocrite within. Jesus commanded this personal introspection when he told the crowd that was about to stone the woman caught in adultery, "He that is without sin among you, let him first cast a stone at her."[6]

Certainly our Lord knows us better than we know ourselves. When He admonished us,

And if the blind lead the blind, both shall fall into the ditch (Matthew 15:14b),

He was warning us of the arrogance of assuming that we know better than others. Paul gave us similar advice when he said,

But they measuring themselves by themselves, and comparing themselves among themselves, are not wise (2 Corinthians 10:12b).

When God moves in our revival meetings, very often He shows people themselves, pictures they rarely see. This supernatural shock treatment usually leads to repentance. David said,

I thought on my ways, and turned my feet unto Thy testimonies. I made haste, and delayed not to keep Thy commandments (Psalm 119:59-60).

The only one who should be throwing accusations at believers is the devil and his bunch. God actually expects that kind of language to come from him. He has nicknamed him the "accuser of the brethren."[7] His punishment is already decreed in the Book. If you are continually critical of your brethren and your mouth spews out critical comments and accusations, I think you'd better ask yourself, "*Which master am I serving with my thoughts and words?*" You may need to be delivered from a critical spirit, my friend. If you are devouring your brothers and sisters with your tongue, you have yielded your member to evil! Stop judging. Repent. You will see brassy heavens shatter.

Obstacle #5: Ignoring the Poor
When you open your heart to the needy,
God opens the heavens to you.

One of the most stinging accusations leveled at the Church to-day is that she has abandoned the poor and needy to the government. It stings because it is for the most part true. No matter what the federal government has done in the past or plans to do in the future, God has not suspended or revoked our obligation to care for the poor! Solomon warned,

Whoso stoppeth his ears at the cry of the poor, he also shall cry himself,
but shall not be heard (Proverbs 21:13).

This is a sobering statement. I don't know about you, but I never want to be in a situation where God will not hear my cry.

The first major conflict in the new church at Jerusalem in-volved its ministry to needy widows and orphans. This conflict wouldn't happen in most of our churches today, but this is nothing to brag about. It wouldn't happen because we don't care for our widows or orphans. We dump them in the unloving arms of government welfare agencies and the weary arms of the Roman Catholic Church and other overloaded benevolent agencies.

On an individual level, most Christians are so insulated from contact with the poor that they don't even know *how* to reach out to the needy! In truth, we know nothing about the daily struggles of the homeless and are not sure we even want to know. If we think at all about the lonely and sometimes desperate lives elderly widows often lead, we quickly dismiss such unhappy thoughts and ponder less disturbing subjects. Or we may shake our heads and say, "Oh my, that's such a shame," every time we see a child who has lost one or both parents to accidents, war, or sickness, but our compassion pretty much stops right there. Instead of reaching out to that unfortunate child, we are happy to gather up our own kids and hurry back home to the safety of our cocoon, far from the cry-ing needs of the poor and destitute.

There is a reason we feel so touched when we meet a needy person. The Spirit of God within us rouses our sleepy senses and urges us to action. Every Scripture we have ever read about caring for the hurting assails us with fresh imagery and power, and every stereotype we have crafted about the poor shames us as it falls to the ground. Suddenly we realize that the poor are simply people who need more than they have. They are struggling just to survive, let alone thrive. The truth is that if Jesus walked the earth today, we would more likely find Him with the poor than inside our church doors.

Look again at the Scripture in Proverbs 21:13:
Whoso stoppeth his ears at the cry of the poor, he also shall cry himself, but shall not be heard.
What a powerful Scripture. How we treat the poor has a vital impact on whether we are heard on high!

God describes the poor in many ways, and He always does it with compassion. The Lord never expects us to cast away all else and make the care of the poor our only priority; but He does expect us to heed the cries of the poor when He leads them into our path. Even Jesus ministered only to those His Father chose, even if this meant that most of the people in a crowd did not receive healing or deliverance. Still, at other times, as the Scriptures tell us, He ministered to all:
Now when the sun was setting, all they that had any sick with divers diseases brought them unto Him; and He laid His hands on every one of them, and healed them (Luke 4:40).

Most churches are geared to minister only to those poor people who need clothing, food, or a one-time loan of cash to tide them over. The problem this presents is that many people who are really poor can't be helped merely by a single handout. Like our Master, we have to walk among them, comfort them, eat meals with them, and minister to them as equals before lasting results are seen. Some can be rescued from poverty through the regeneration of their spirits and the renewal of their minds with the Word of God. Others need tangible aid in addition to this regeneration, since their earthly source of income has been lost through death or disease. Then the Church needs to shoulder the permanent responsibility of providing for their needs. This is what the church body at Jerusalem was doing for the widows and orphans in their midst.

This may not sound like the usual revival talk, but I tell you it is Bible talk. The revived Church is a caring Church. The revived believer is a serving believer.

Obstacle #6: Teaching the Commandments of Men
**When we are willing to turn from the precepts of men,
we see the commandments of God breaking through cloudy skies.**

Many believers around the country pray ineffectively and live in continual frustration and discouragement because they have believed the commandments of men rather than the doctrines of God.

*This people draweth nigh unto Me with their mouth, and honoureth Me with their lips; but their heart is far from Me. But in vain they do worship Me, **teaching for doctrines the commandments of men*** (Matthew 15:8-9).

Many of the commandments represented in our churches as doctrines virtually require Christians to disallow or recast the Word of God as revealed in the Book of Acts, in First and Second Corinthians, in Ephesians, and even in the Gospels. Entire sections of these inspired books are prefaced by a familiar chorus of buts as anxious Bible teachers and preachers scramble to reassure their audiences that these things passed away with the apostles—which they did not—as if they were *limited* to the ministry of the apostles. It seems that everything that has anything to do with a *supernatural God* who does *supernatural works* in our day is systematically purged to conform with the tidy commandments of men.

This same litany goes on in Charismatic and Pentecostal churches. Here ministers disregard certain Bible verses that seem to conflict with their favorite man-made commandments about the end times, the Trinity, communion, baptism, or whatever dress code is in force at the time. My friend, the truth is that the God of revival cares nothing for the commandments of men, but He dearly loves every man. He longs to see His river flow through the hearts of everyone who calls on the name of His Son.

This will not happen as long as many Christians confuse doctrinal belief with genuine experience. There is a huge difference. Just because you have been raised in a Pentecostal or Charismatic tradition does not mean that you have experienced the presence and power of God. Many who have heard about it and believe in it, have never experienced it.

On the other hand, many good Christians have the misdirected belief that doing things in decency and in order means rigidly regulating worship and banning all manifestations of spirituality or emotion. This misplaced zeal has produced powerless, lifeless churches where the supernatural gifts of the Spirit described in the Epistles are completely missing. A Church without power is unable to reap and keep the harvest of souls in this last generation. God is not pleased with extra-biblical doctrines that promote "...a form of godliness, but denying the power thereof."[8] Jesus said we would have *power*—not boredom—when the Holy Ghost comes upon us.

I am sure that the arrival of the Holy Spirit in the Upper Room didn't exactly match our modern definitions of decently and in order, but it was God nevertheless. I know that in my case, I wasn't prepared to accept the freedom revival would ultimately bring to Brownsville Assembly of God Church, so God dealt with me until I changed. He touched me so powerfully that I lay helpless in front of my own congregation for the entire length of each service. This went on for over a month when the revival first began! When God finally let me stand before the congregation again, I had put my pointer finger back in my pocket where it belonged.

Roadblock #7: Self-condemnation
You must remember who you are.
The lies of the enemy cannot condemn the sons of God.

Satan is called "the accuser of the brethren"[9] for good reason. Just when we think we have left every distraction behind and have shut the door to our bedrooms, offices, and prayer closets, a familiar accusing voice begins to rehearse all our faults and failures in agonizing detail. We need to remember this wise bit of advice: Consider the source. Any time you go past the talk stage and truly separate yourself from your daily routine for a time of focused prayer in God's presence, your accuser is waiting. He will do anything to keep you from praying, with condemnation being his favorite tactic. The surprising fact is that if satan should ever take a holiday, we would probably continue his condemning work without his help! This may be why John the apostle said:

> *And hereby we know that we are of the truth, and shall assure our hearts before Him. For if our heart condemn us, God is greater than our heart, and knoweth all things. Beloved, if our heart condemn us not, then have we confidence toward God. And whatsoever we ask, we receive of Him, because we keep His commandments, and do those things that are pleasing in His sight* (1 John 3:19-22).

The first thing you should do when you come before God in prayer is to *assure* yourself of your standing before Him. Remind yourself that Jesus Christ alone has qualified you to enter the presence of God. Ask the Holy Spirit to reveal any unconfessed sin that might be blocking your direct communication with God, and then confess it and repent. Begin to praise God and recall some of the verses from His Word that declare your identity in Christ. Rejoice in God's Word and declare:

> I am the righteousness of God in Christ. I am a new creature, created in God's image for His good pleasure. I am a child of God and an heir of all the promises through Christ Jesus. Greater is He that is in me than he that is in the world! Now there is no condemnation against me because I am in Christ Jesus, and I walk after the Spirit and not after the flesh.[10]

Obstacle #8: Disrespect to Spouse
Suppressing the anointing and gifts in your spouse will rob you of the full power needed to break through brassy heavens.

> *Likewise, ye husbands, dwell with* [your wives] *according to knowledge, giving honour unto the wife, as unto the weaker vessel, and as*

*being heirs together of the grace of life; **that your prayers be not hindered*** (1 Peter 3:7).

Many marriages are destroyed and much prayer is hindered when the easy familiarity of long-term marital relationships spawns contempt. Although contempt born from familiarity is quite commonplace in our world, this tendency need not destroy our homes. Love and genuine concern expressed by each member of a well-kept marriage do much to keep this destroyer away.

When, however, marriage partners begin to take each other for granted, forgetting the small gestures that show love and appreciation, a gradual contempt may begin to grow silently day by day. It is especially easy for men to treat their wives with rudeness and outright disrespect, since they often have the dominant personality in the home.

This is not God's plan. Man is woman's protector, not her destroyer. Everything he does should build her up, not tear her down. This should be true of his attitudes, his words, and his actions as he shows gentle consideration for her needs and her personal wishes. Praise will earn him respect much sooner than selfish domination. Careful listening and thoughtful kindnesses will turn her heart toward him.

Too often, however, marriages are torn apart by judgments and assumptions that breed contempt. Beware lest satan, using his most compelling lie against you, implants in your mind the thought that your spouse does not recognize or appreciate your anointing and the destiny God has placed on your life. This lie tears at the fabric of your spiritual strength and the very beliefs that identify you as a believer. Once the enemy has convinced you that your spouse does not share deeply in your life and work, you begin to follow a dangerous path that separates you from your spouse—even while you live under the same roof! These separate life paths will most certainly result in tragic pain, and may even lead to separation and divorce.

The heavens are brass over those who are willing to accept such demonic lies. Every other temptation waits for its turn to humiliate and destroy the one who separates from his or her spouse because of ministry and calling. Strength is drained and the safety and protection of the family unit is compromised. Temptation, sickness, depression, discouragement, rebellion, and even disobedience among your children may all result from this breach.

Trust is gone and the help-mate principle no longer functions. Now an ominous sense of loneliness and abandonment creeps into the heart of every family member, and there is no longer a sense of destiny and hope. Inevitably, the bond of love and safety that once ruled the household fades into nothing more than memory.

Of course I understand that in a very few and rare cases, the separated spouse does not want to accept the call of God on the other spouse's life. Do not assume that this is true for you. In the vast majority of marriages where separation occurs because of ministry and calling, one spouse has simply believed the lie that his partner does not have what it takes to walk where the "anointed spouse" must walk. Although this problem is prevalent and can be found in both sides of a marriage, it is most often the woman who is the target of this vicious attack.

Safeguard your marriage by recognizing that differences in perspective and calling do not necessarily mean that your spouse does not support you. Be careful not to let assumptions about your spouse's commitment to you, your ministry, or Christ rob you of the blessings and joys committed marriage partners can find. Two are always stronger than one. Value and safeguard that strength, being attentive to the needs and giftings of each marriage partner. Above all, pray together. Couples who pray together discover much about themselves, their marriage, and their ministries that they would not otherwise learn. Then trust God to safeguard your hearts and minds. In so doing you will keep the skies over your home clear and open.

Hunger and Prayer

Hunger for "more of God" is at the heart of truly effective prayer. It seems that the more you seek God, the more you desire Him. Yet this hunger of the heart will also draw the most depraved man and the most hardened backslider to the altar of God. If your life is entangled with one or more of the obstacles discussed here, take heart. Your hunger for more has brought you this far. It will take you the rest of the way to wholeness if you will yield to each gentle tug on your heart by the Holy Spirit.

This hunger for more has drawn ministers and believers from virtually every denomination and theological camp in the world to seek the face of God in this revival at Brownsville. I am happy to say that many, if not most of them, return to their churches and homes immersed in God's glory with a totally different perspective of revival and the importance of persistent prayer. The reports continue to pour into our offices concerning the great move of God in both traditional and non-traditional, denominational and non-denominational, churches. Most of them have felt a fresh and urgent call to prayer. God doesn't look at our titles and ministerial credentials; He looks at our hearts. Now He is trying to teach us how to do the same.

Endnotes

1. See Matthew 21:13.
2. See 1 Samuel 2:12–4:22.
3. James Strong, *The Comprehensive Concordance to the Bible*, (Iowa Falls, IA: World Bible Publishers, n.d.), **regard** (Heb., #7200).
4. Ibid.
5. See 1 Corinthians 12:11.
6. John 8:7b.
7. Revelation 12:10.
8. 2 Timothy 3:5.
9. Revelation 12:10.
10. See 2 Corinthians 5:21,17; Genesis 1:26; Revelation 4:11; Romans 8:16-17; 1 John 4:4; Romans 8:1.

Chapter 4

Cleanse the Waters So the River Will Flow

**I believe that an uncontrolled sex drive
is the greatest hindrance to a man's prayer life.**

For three weekends in a row, a striking blonde woman walked into the service with a couple I had never seen before. Even though the three were visibly touched by the Spirit of God during the services, they didn't come down to receive Christ. I wanted to meet them, but they left so quickly after each service that I just couldn't reach them in time. They vanished after the third Sunday, and I turned my thoughts toward the ongoing ministry at the church.

Several months later, on the exact day I had finished a 13-day fast, my executive assistant, Rose Compton, knocked on my office door and said, "Pastor, we have an emergency out here. Do you have a few moments to see this lady?" I knew by the look on Rose's face that something was seriously wrong, so I told her to bring the lady in.

When the woman entered my office, I was appalled by the look of death I saw on her face. Her face was ashen-gray, her blonde hair was unkempt and in disarray, her sunken eyes were dull and red-rimmed, and it was clear she was in torment. I knew I had never met her before, but there was something familiar about her appearance. Then I remembered her: This was the blonde woman who had come to the Sunday services months before! Now I barely recognized her.

After Rose introduced the visitor, I said, "I think I remember you from some of our Sunday services. Didn't you come a while back with a redheaded woman and her husband?"

"Yes, Pastor, that was me. I just wish I had never left."

"What happened to you? Are you okay?" The young woman's eyes filled with tears.

She told me that one rainy night weeks after she had stopped coming to our church, she was driving along a deserted stretch of highway when she saw a young woman walking alone beside the road. She felt sorry for the woman, so she stopped and offered her a ride. She ended up taking the hitchhiker home, where she fed her, got her some dry clothes, and tried to comfort her.

The young woman in my office looked down for a moment, then said, "I don't know how it happened. I've never had any thoughts or desires in this direction, but somehow she seduced me and we ended up in bed together in a lesbian relationship." This woman had been a virgin up until that time, but the hitchhiker managed to manipulate the young woman's well-meaning desire to comfort and help. She looked up at me in her shame and said, "I'll never forget what she said when it was over. As she left the room, she looked back at me and said, 'Oh, by the way, I'm a witch.' Something sinister immediately crept over me."

From that night on, the woman's life quickly fell apart. By allowing herself to be seduced into having lesbian relations with the witch, she had opened up her life to demonic oppression. Evil spirits began to come at her right through her bedroom wall in the middle of the night. The near constant torment made her unable to sleep. Then she lost her appetite. Finally she began to lose any desire or ability to take care of herself.

The enemy realized that this young woman was almost ready to receive Christ after her visits to the church, so he ordered a principality, an architect of evil, to hatch a plan and lay the trap. He connived to make the heavens over her head brass. As a result, this woman nearly lost her soul, and possibly her life.

In the end, she came to the church because that was the one place where she knew she could find help. She wanted to be free, so I led her in a prayer of repentance, and she received Jesus Christ as her Lord. Then the battle began. The power of the Holy Ghost flowed through me like a river that day because of the fast I had just completed. The Holy Spirit used me to cast some powerful demons out of the woman, after which she renounced all ties to the dark world. It was the grace of *God* that satan hadn't snuffed out her life before she found deliverance through Jesus Christ. She had almost waited too long.

My friend, satan has spent thousands of years perfecting his traps, snares, and enticements. The Bible says that we are not ignorant of his devices.[1] Still, most Christians act like they *are immune to the wiles of the evil one*, when they are not. Fewer believers would underestimate or dismiss satan's devices if they knew the secret to his success: He uses *our own desires and lusts* as bait to lure us into his snares in the same way that a deer hunter uses musk, scents, or salt licks to attract bucks to a deer stand.

One Obstacle Confronts Us All

This is why I believe that the greatest hindrance to a man's prayer life is an uncontrolled sex drive, which in turn causes problems for the woman in his life. I am not talking about some isolated problem that affects only a few people. I believe that more than 80 percent of all Christians above the age of 12 struggle with some aspect of their sexual desires every day. (The remainder may not experience as many challenges in this area because they have experienced a significant drop in their sexual drive due to advanced age or physical problems.)

Brassy skies are the inevitable consequence whenever we yield to these temptations to unlawfully exploit the sexual desires God meant for good. If our response to these desires hinders our prayer, it also helps satan to thicken the skies over our heads. Thus our struggles with sexual desire can affect our walk with God, as well as our marriages, our finances, and our churches. I am convinced that very few people understand the consequences of violating God's Word concerning sexual activity.

God said,

> *Therefore shall a man leave his father and his mother, and shall cleave unto his wife: and they shall be one flesh* (Genesis 2:24).

The Hebrew word for "cleave" is *dabaq*; it means "to be joined together as in sexual intercourse."[2] Paul repeated this Old Testament passage in Greek in his letter to the Ephesians. The English translation reads,

> *For this cause shall a man leave his father and mother, and shall be joined unto his wife, and they two shall be one flesh* (Ephesians 5:31).

The Greek word for "joined" is *proskollao*, which means "to be adhered to," referring to deep intimacy. The first part of the word, *pros*, means "forward to, toward" and *kollao* means "to glue."[3] God made man and woman to *proskollao*, to blend in sexual union face to face so their spirits and their bodies will blend together in spiritual and physical intimacy. Within the bond of marriage, this produces an ecstatic blending of spirits and souls that involves our total beings.

In contrast, the Greek word describing the mating of animals is *kollao*. This refers to a sexual act that is not performed face to face. It is nothing more than a physical mating. Dogs, horses, and other animals move casually from one sex partner to another during mating season. Although some species tend to have one mate for life, they procreate through *kollao*, a sexual act that has no spiritual effect.

A man receives much more from his mate than a physical release. He receives a deep sense of nurturing, spiritual replenishment, and refreshment in union with her. A woman receives a deep sense of security as she draws from her husband's love. She is nurtured through caring intimacy with her husband and protector. Sex is intensely personal and pleasurable, and it is all part of God's plan. However, when uncontrolled men *kollao* like animals, they violate God's plan and suffer severe consequences.

> *What? know ye not that he which is **joined** to a harlot is **one body**? for two, saith he, shall be one flesh. But he that is joined unto the Lord is one spirit. Flee fornication. Every sin that a man doeth is without the body; but he that committeth fornication sinneth against his own body* (1 Corinthians 6:16-18).

Sex Is Like a Camera

Sex works just like the eye in a camera. When the shutter release button is pushed, the eye inside snaps open and whatever enters through the lens of that camera is exposed on the film. If that camera has been aimed and deliberately focused, it can produce a beautiful picture of a rose, a carnation, a sunset, a snow-covered mountain, or a beautiful glacier. In fact, cameras were made to be centered on an object or person and focused precisely, so they can produce beautiful pictures to be enjoyed for a lifetime.

On the other hand, what happens if you haphazardly swing the camera and fire off shot after shot? What happens if you accidentally shoot a picture just as you put it into your pocket? The camera shutter will automatically go click, and whatever is captured on the lens in that moment—such as a blurry shot of the carpet—will be permanently exposed on the film inside. If a camera is used indiscriminately, whatever the lens of the camera is exposed to will be developed on the film.

In human intercourse, the "lens" in the spirits of the man and the woman open automatically and are exposed to everything that is in the other person. The Bible says that we become "one" with whomever we join with.[4] If a man joins with a prostitute, he literally becomes "one" with her—and with every other partner she has ever had! Even the world has had to face the unpleasant fact that a sexually promiscuous person can pass along every sexually transmitted disease his or her partners have ever picked up along the way. In the age of deadly sexually transmitted diseases like the AIDS virus, millions of people have discovered this too late. In a similar manner, when the blonde woman was seduced by the witch, the "shutter" of

her spirit automatically opened and she was exposed to the demonic forces at work in that witch. Until the blood of Jesus
cleansed her, the heavens over her head turned to brass and her
life became hell on earth.

How Is Sex Supposed to Work?

God intends for a man and woman to be engaged or betrothed
for awhile. The word *betrothed* means that you have promised and
reserved yourself for marriage to another person of the opposite
sex. This should be a period of time during which you begin to
study your intended mate and find out what kind of background
he or she has.

If you are a man, you should ask yourself, "How has my fiancée
been brought up? Is she good wife material? Does she have the
makings of a homemaker? Does she know how to cook? Is she too
tied to her mother to move away if the need arises? Will she run to
Daddy every time a decision needs to be made?" Check out her
character and see if there is any spiritual pollution in her family.

If you are a woman, you should ask yourself, "Is there witchcraft, fortune-telling, or astrology in his family background? Does
alcoholism, drug abuse, or physical abuse run in the family? What
was he taught about God? What does he think about child rearing
and discipline in the home? Will he make a good father and priest
over our home?"

You may say, "Isn't love all we need? Why is this so important?" This is important because when you join together sexually
on your wedding night, the lens of your spirit will open and you
will be bonded to whatever your spouse is. Whatever is in your
spirit will also flow back into your marriage partner. Every person
your spouse has been with, everything he or she believes, and all
the darkness that surrounds him or her will be linked with and
bonded to *you!* Intercourse is not just a physical act. The whole of
who you are is transferred during sexual union. This is why God
ordained that one woman join with one man for life. This is also
why repentance and deliverance are so essential before marriage.

The blood of Jesus cleanses you from sin and washes your spirit from the pollution of your past. If you know that there is this kind of history in your life or in your future spouse's life, it is so much better to find repentance arïd deliverance before marriage. You need fresh film in your camera, so let the Holy Spirit put all the other negative things under the blood.

Many couples, however, are married for years before they discover how their past is affecting their marriage relationship. It is never too late to repent of those old skeletons that still rattle in your closet. It is never too late for the Holy Spirit to release you from those old demonic influences. The sooner they are dealt with, the sooner the Lord Jesus can begin the healing process, restoring your marriage to the satisfying covenant God intended it to be.

The fulfillment found in the marriage bed is essential for your well-being. Since you lose part of yourself when you give yourself in sex to someone, God arranged for you to find what you lost in the countenance or face of your beloved. One reason you are to join together face to face is that God made human beings with a "countenance." The human face has the unique ability to display the glory of God. Only human beings were made with this capacity—not a donkey, a rhino, a zebra, or an elephant. No other animal was made with this special potential to display the glory of God. When Moses came down from the mountain, he had to veil his face because of the glory of God on his countenance![5]

We are like reflectors or mirrors in a marriage relationship. Our faces reflect what is in our spirits. Whether we are sad, glad, worried, or pleased, this is expressed through our countenance. When we lose ourselves in sexual union, it is reflected back to us as love, satisfaction, and confidence. When there is no one there for us to love, be committed to, and reflect, we are lonely and we feel the deficiency. If a relationship is not in the bonds of matrimony, we can't receive what we need. It is blocked by sin.

If you walk into the average American classroom filled with teenagers in the 7th through the 12th grade, you will notice that many of them just don't care about anything anymore. They have skipped the discipline of eating a balanced meal and have gratified themselves with desserts and junk foods. Now they are terminally bored. Their attire is sloppy, they are probably overweight, they've lost their zest for life, and some of them are even suicidal. Why? They became sexually active at a young age. They've been involved in the *kollao* mating process—they've mated like animals solely for a physical thrill and hormonal release—with no thought of cleaving for life. They've known only the temporary relationship inspired by lust, not the covenant relationship motivated by lifelong commitment to somebody in the marriage bed. They've given themselves away to virtual strangers, and each time they lose something with no hope of receiving back what they lost through the countenance of a spouse in holy wedlock. They are dying of loneliness, and they know that something is missing, but they don't know what. This is why those of us in the ministry must not shy away from telling with boldness the truth regarding illicit sexual activities.

Each time these young people engage in *kollao*, they lose a bit more of their self-esteem and their pride. Although they feel unfulfilled and insecure, they usually will not face the truth of their loss. "Hey, I'm sexually active," they say. "I ought to be happy. They call me the stud of the school, but why am I so unhappy? Why have I been drinking so hard lately?" These teens are trying to drown their troubles with alcohol and mood-altering drugs because they are reaping the repercussions of choosing to abandon God's way of living.

It is the same story with the "glitteratti" and the so-called "beautiful people" in the entertainment capitals of Hollywood, Nashville, and New York City. They have fame, talent, popularity, money, and the sexual favors of almost anybody they want. Why are they snorting cocaine until they can't function on stage and in front of the camera? Why are they drinking so hard that they end their careers in jail or in the arms of a prostitute? It is because you can't defy God's Word without paying a price. Remember, God has life fixed so it won't work without Christ. Sin always comes with built-in consequences. If you sin, you will have hell to pay. Heaven will become brass.

God's Plan Takes More Than "Good Plumbing"

The animal sex act isn't unique; it is just a matter of having plumbing that works. Even mindless dogs can do it. It doesn't take brains, commitment, or a single good character attribute—the things needed to be good parents and lifelong mates. God has a better plan, and it is exciting and rewarding. He commands us to leave and cleave for life.[6]

My precious wife, Brenda, has always made me feel secure in her love. She makes me feel like I am the best thing that ever happened to her, when in reality, she is the best thing that ever happened to me. I am not interested in *anybody* else, and I know that she doesn't want anybody else but me. There is security, joy, fulfillment, and happiness in our relationship. We were both virgins when we married many years ago, and our marriage relationship has been one of joy and fulfillment because we've done things God's way.

Now if I were to go out and yield to temptation to have an affair with somebody, several things would happen. First of all, I would be hit with guilt so strong that it would paralyze every aspect of my life. Second, I would be violating everything that matters the most to me: my relationship with God, my body, my marriage trust, Brenda, and my children. Third, I would begin to suffer. My finances would suffer, as would my health—since the Bible says that a dart would shoot through my liver![7] The Hebrew word for "liver" is *kabed,* or "heavy," since the liver is the heaviest of the internal organs.[8] It comes from the root word, *kabod,* which is the word for "glory." Could it be that God is saying if we join with a harlot or adulterer, that a dart will be shot through our glory?

If you are facing the temptation to have sex before marriage or outside of marriage, ask yourself this question: "Is it really worth it?" I know you want to say, "Oh, but when you're tempted and when you're hot, it's hard to say you're not interested." My friend, your body may say, "Go for it," but neither your body nor the devil will tell you the truth. Sexual sin brings a shame and reproach that will stay with you for the rest of your days. Remember, your hormones have no conscience!

Avoid Sexual Entanglement

A young man stood before our congregation in a revival service and told the following story. He testified that God had called him to be an evangelist, but when he went off to Bible school for training, his friends began to ridicule him. He ended up dropping out of Bible school, after which he got entangled in pornography and sexual sin. So far had he fallen that he had given up his dream of preaching the gospel. Thank God he was drawn to the revival, where he repented of his sin. The sad thing is that he didn't have to fall into sin in the first place. If I've heard that kind of testimony one time, I've heard it a thousand times. For every one who is recovered and restored to the Kingdom, there are countless others who never escape satan's snare.

Modern America has become a beehive of illicit sexual escapades. You may be a blood-washed believer, but once you walk out of the confines of your godly home, you are susceptible to temptation that could lead to sin. Don't be ignorant of satan's devices. You may say, "Oh Brother Kilpatrick, you're preaching to the wrong person." No, I'm preaching to the right person. Nobody is exempt.

I remember the time a preacher got up at a conference and said, "Bless God, there is one thing I'll never do. I'll never be unfaithful to my bride." Before the next conference came around, he had fallen into sexual sin. Beware of haughty declarations that you cannot fulfill. Walk humbly before God. Live cautiously and lean on the Lord with all of your being. Paul said,

> For I say, through the grace given unto me, to every man that is among you, not to think of himself more highly than he ought to think... (Romans 12:3).

We are saved and preserved by grace, not by willpower or performance, my friend. This is especially important for men because of the strong sex drive God has given them.

The *Waters* of Human Sexuality in the Bible

The Bible speaks of our human sexuality in terms of "waters." The Book of Proverbs refers to a cistern, a well, and a fountain:

*Drink **waters** out of thine own **cistern**, and running waters out of thine own **well**. Let thy **fountains** be dispersed abroad, and rivers of water in the streets. Let them be thine own, and not strangers' with thee. Let thy **fountain** be blessed: and rejoice with the wife of thy youth* (Proverbs 5:15-18).

1. *The Virgin: A Cistern of Untapped Water*
    The Bible depicts a virgin as a "cistern," which is an untapped well. Her pure waters are sealed until the day of her marriage. When she marries a man who has committed his life to her, she allows him to uncover her well and drink of her waters. Once a virgin marries and becomes sexually active with her husband, she is considered a "well."

2. *The Married Woman: A Well of Refreshing Water for Her Husband*
    A married woman, like a well, is a deep cistern that is continually filled with deep, still, refreshing water. She take pleasure in intimacy. In fact, this is what she enjoys the most about her relationship with her husband: the intimacy, the sweetness, and the kindness he shows her. Thus when the Scriptures refer to "drinking waters out of your own cistern," they are telling you to have sex with your own mate.

3. *The Married Man: A Fountain*
    A man has a strong sex drive, much like a fountain is a stream of water driven by an internal force. When he is sexually active with his wife, he most enjoys the release of this strong drive.

When both partners in a marriage are allowed to flow together within the relationship as God designed it, their sexual union brings both the man and the woman *satisfaction* and *ecstasy*. Both are refreshed, renewed, strengthened, and reassured in their love for one another. If, however, the marriage bed is forsaken for whatever reason, both are put at risk.

The man is at the greatest risk because of the very strong force of his sexual drive. He needs sexual relations with his wife on a regular basis. The woman, on the other hand, is at risk when her spouse withholds the intimacy and gentle caring she needs. This is why Paul the apostle warned Christian couples,

> *Nevertheless, to avoid fornication, let every man have his own wife, and let every woman have her own husband. Let the husband render unto the wife due benevolence: and likewise also the wife unto the husband. The wife hath not power of her own body, but the husband: and likewise also the husband hath not power of his own body, but the wife. Defraud ye not one the other* [don't withhold sexual relations], *except it be with consent for a time, that ye may give yourselves to fasting and prayer; and come together again, that Satan tempt you not for your incontinency* (1 Corinthians 7:2-5).

Stolen Waters: Sex Outside Marriage

Long before there was any medical knowledge about venereal diseases or the spiritual laws of transference, the Bible perfectly described the symptoms of sexual sin. Proverbs 23:27 says,

> *For a whore is a deep ditch; and a strange woman is a narrow pit.*

Now a "deep ditch" and a "narrow pit" are not exactly sweet metaphors for purity and refreshment in sexual activity. The water in a ditch is diseased water, and the water in a narrow pit is contaminated and polluted. All kinds of insects and diseases brood and breed there.

The Book of Proverbs also likens sex with a prostitute to "stolen waters."

> *A foolish woman is clamorous: she is simple, and knoweth nothing. ...she saith to him, Stolen waters are sweet, and bread eaten in secret is pleasant. But he knoweth not that the dead are there; and that her guests are in the depths of hell* (Proverbs 9:13,16-18).

In other words, sex with a prostitute or an adulteress is like partaking of impure, polluted, and disease-filled water that brings sickness and death.

God said that a pure woman is a well, but a whore is a deep ditch and an adulteress is a narrow pit. God planned for women to be only pure cisterns and refreshing wells. He ordained for every man to be a pure fountain, dedicated totally to one cistern and well for life. He created the reproductive organs of mankind and set certain laws into motion to govern our relationships. If we deviate from what He has ordained, we reap automatic, built-in consequences. God doesn't have to lean over His throne and say, "I caught you." Just like He put the laws of gravity into effect on the earth, He set into place the laws that govern human sexuality. If you try to defy gravity by jumping from a high place, you will be seriously injured or killed. In the same way, if you defy God's plan for sexual behavior, you will have the devil to pay.

"What I do sexually is my business and nobody else's!" Don't believe it. The Bible says,

For the ways of man are before the eyes of the Lord, and He pondereth all his goings (Proverbs 5:21).

Pensacola is a Navy town, and we have worked with military personnel for many years. When sailors finally step from the deck of their ship in Italy or Hawaii after an unbroken tour of several months at sea, their hormones are raging. Many of them go looking for a place of sexual release, thinking that their time with a prostitute or a mistress is "just a sex act." It is not. When these sailors come home, they soon discover that they are different. Although they don't understand why, they are anxious and worked up, and they feel lonely and depressed. They wonder why they are no longer happy with their wives and children.

These sailors' problem is that they bonded sexually and spiritually with prostitutes, complete strangers in distant lands. Not only are they now bonded to these prostitutes, but these young men are also bonded to the countless other sex partners these strangers have had. My friend, it really messes you up when you are unfaithful sexually.

If you are a Christian, you know that God traces sin right to your heart and your most private thoughts. He knows when you are deviating from your spiritual walk, when you are being tempted and seduced. Temptation is not sin; but if you start pondering and fantasizing about committing fornication or being unfaithful to your wife, you're guilty.

Jesus said,

...whosoever looketh on a woman to lust after her hath committed adultery with her already in his heart (Matthew 5:28).

This does not mean that since you've already thought of the sin, you should go through with it. Both the thought and the action are wrong, but until the sin is physically accomplished, you have sinned against God. Afterward, you have sinned against yourself. You have tasted stolen waters, thereby violating your wife, your family, and your own body. Stop every temptation at the thought stage. If you harbor and savor the temptation in your imagination long enough, it will become a stronghold.

The apostle Paul gave us the best advice: "Flee...youthful lusts."[9] This means you should run away or escape from lustful thoughts or situations. Our evangelist, Stephen Hill, has said many times, "If you are out driving and you see a body jogging toward you, don't look to see if it's male or female. If you want your anointing to leave, friend, if you want the power of God to leave you like a bird flying from a perch, you just start fantasizing and being led away by your own lust." I guarantee that the glory and anointing you have sought for so long will leave you in a split second if you grieve the Holy Spirit by clinging to a lustful sin. Sexual pleasure is not worth it.

People get involved in sexual sins for several reasons that we need to know about. First, they are curious. Many affairs begin with the illicit thought, "I wonder what it would be like with her?" Second, they become bored and restless. "My marriage is boring," a man says. "Once my wife had a few children, she lost her shape and build." Friend, if that's the only reason you married her, your relationship won't last long. God never intended for you to choose a wife or a husband predicated on how he or she looks! Beauty is only skin deep, and skin changes with every passing year. What is going to happen if your wife has a mastectomy, or if your husband loses an arm in an accident? Will these things all of a sudden make your marriage vows null and void?

The Temptations Provoked by a Loose Woman

A man of God must go out of his way to avoid the temptations of loose women. They pose such a danger to a man's holy walk before God that the Bible devotes many verses to warn us about the dangerous ways of evil women. A loose woman is a prostitute, an adulteress, or any other woman who will not make good "wife material." Not every girl you date is going to make a good wife. She may be a bombshell in the looks department, but that doesn't mean she would make a good wife or mother. She may be built just exactly like your fantasy wants her to be built, but what about her character? She could lead you straight to hell. Cities like New Orleans and other pleasure cities have fallen under tremendous demonic influence because of the seductive wiles of loose women and the unbridled sexual desires of men. The Book of Proverbs says,

> *And, behold, there met him a woman with the attire of an harlot, and subtle of heart. (She is loud and stubborn; her feet abide not in her house: now is she without, now in the streets, and lieth in wait at every corner.) So she caught him, and kissed him, and with an impudent face said unto him, I have peace offerings with me; this day have I payed my vows. Therefore came I forth to meet thee, diligently to seek thy face, and I have found thee. I have decked my bed with coverings of tapestry, with carved works, with fine linen of Egypt. I have perfumed my bed with myrrh, aloes, and cinnamon. Come, let us take our fill of love until the morning: let us solace ourselves with loves. For the goodman is not at home, he is gone a long journey: he hath taken a bag of money with him, and will come home at the day appointed. With her much fair speech she caused him to yield, with the flattering of her lips she forced him* (Proverbs 7:10-21).

This Scripture passage shows the various snares a loose woman will use to trap a man.

1. A loose woman catches a man's eyes by dressing seductively, carefully exposing parts of her body with low-cut blouses and seductive skirts. She walks and moves in overtly sexual ways.

2. A loose woman shocks a man by talking about intimacy without inhibition. Verse 13 of Proverbs chapter 7 describes a bold woman who caught a man and kissed him passionately with lips that were burning hot with lust. She shocked him by talking about taboo subjects, such as his ability to make love. Her seductive words set his hormones on fire.

3. A loose woman reassures a man, saying, "God put us together." Many a man of God has fallen into sexual sin right in the church building after agreeing to counsel women *alone* in his office because these women said, "God told me to come to you right away. You are the only one who can help me with my problem and I just can't wait any longer..." The woman in Proverbs 7 bragged that she had just paid her debt for sin under the old covenant law. She had just been to the church of her day.

4. A loose woman tempts a man with stories about how sexy her bed looks and how her room smells. She goes on to describe in vivid detail just what it would be like to make love to her.

5. A loose woman uses words of flattery and invitation to secure what she wants once she has painted a picture of desire and inflamed a man's sexual desire:

   Come, let us take our fill of love until the morning (Proverbs 7:18a).

   With her much fair speech she caused him to yield, with the flattering of her lips she forced him (Proverbs 7:21).

A married man whose wife continually refreshes and builds up his fragile ego will not be as susceptible to this tactic of evil.

6. A loose woman finally tells a man, "We won't get caught. My husband is out of town."

An evil woman views sex as a game of power. She is driven by demonic genius to hunt for susceptible men of power and prestige and bend them to her will. She is especially attracted to men of great visibility, such as preachers, politicians, and well-known businessmen. She is not so much driven by sexual desire as by a desire for illicit power over men. Such a woman will actually plot and strategize ways to seduce the man in her sights. She might say, "I bet he'll be mine if I build him up and flatter him just right. He doesn't look like he's too happy at home." Anyone can become the target of a loose woman: the boss, the manager, the evangelist, the pastor, the politician, and the Sunday school teacher. If a man falls into her trap, she destroys his very soul. Look at Proverbs 6:32:

> *But whoso committeth adultery with a woman lacketh understanding:*
> *he that doeth it destroyeth his own soul.*

Any man who commits adultery destroys his mind, his emotions, his body, and his reputation. He will never again be considered an honorable man once his indiscretion is revealed—and it will be. If satan doesn't reveal it with the hope of destroying him, God will, so He can save him. Adultery is a unique crime because it turns a pure relationship into a polluted one. There is more hope for a thief than for an adulterer because a thief can pay back sevenfold what he has stolen.[10] An adulterer can never pay back what he has stolen.

Isn't it interesting that Jesus performed His first miracle at a wedding and that it had to do with water? If you recall the story in John 2:1-10, Jesus and His disciples were invited to a marriage feast in Cana of Galilee. When the guests called for wine when there was no more, Mary told Jesus the problem. He told the servants of the house to fill large water pots with water and take a dipper of the water to the master of the feast.

Obedience Releases the River of God

When those worried servants went to dip water from those large containers, they couldn't see the miracle that was in the waters. It was only when they obeyed and dipped a ladle into the water that it was turned into wine. People don't understand the miracle that God has put in the marriage relationship. It only looks like boring, ordinary water to people who view marriage from outside God's plan. The Lord knows the miracle power that lies hidden in marriage.

When we dip into the waters of marriage God's way, we discover that we are actually drinking the wine of God! When we honor the **well** of the woman and the **fountain** of the man in obedience to God's plan, He releases a third source of "water" into that marriage relationship: the **river** of His Spirit. The Holy Spirit is also symbolized in Scripture as wine. This completes the miraculous picture of the union of the waters of human sexuality and supernatural spirituality in marriage.

Apply this understanding to the woman at the well in John 4:11-42. It was no coincidence that Jesus met this Samaritan woman beside the well of Jacob. Isn't it interesting that when she asked Him to let her drink of His well or fountain that springs up into everlasting life, He told her, "Call your husband and come here," implying, "Where is your fountain?" When she said she had no husband, Jesus answered,

Thou hast well said, I have no husband: for thou hast had five husbands; and he whom thou now hast is not thy husband: in that saidst thou truly (John 4:17b-18).

The good news is that Jesus was telling her, "I have water for you that will take away all your sin and shame." He brought this fallen woman hope and confidence.

Most of us know that the blood of Jesus cleanses us from all sin and all unrighteousness, but consider what Jesus was saying to this sexually polluted woman who wanted to worship God from a pure heart. He told her about a well of water springing up into everlasting life. This implies an artesian well, a well that yields an inexhaustible supply of fresh water from underneath the surface with great force. Jesus was talking about the river of God, the Holy Spirit. Compare this with His words in the Gospel of John:

He that believeth on Me, as the scripture hath said, out of his belly shall flow rivers of living water. (But this spake He of the Spirit, which they that believe on Him should receive...) (John 7:38-39).

God gave us the blood of His only begotten Son to cleanse us from sin in His sight. He also gave us the river of the Holy Ghost to give us power over sin and satan in *this* life! Jesus told the disciples,

But ye shall receive power, after that the Holy Ghost has come upon you (Acts 1:8a).

You need more than cleansing from the sin you have already committed. You need power to overcome the sin you will be tempted to commit today and tomorrow. You need the overwhelming, overcoming, overflowing current of the river of God to flood your banks and refresh your waters that have become polluted through sin.

Bathsheba was the mother of Solomon. She became the wife of David, but only after she committed adultery with David when she was married to another man. When David took her to his bed, Bathsheba became an evil woman and a contaminated well. Thus when Bathsheba announced that she was pregnant, David plotted to hide his sin by bringing her husband home from the war front. When this man refused to sleep with his wife for reasons of honorable duty as a soldier, David plotted his murder.

After Bathsheba's husband died because of David's cold-blooded plot, she married David and bore the son they conceived in adultery. When the child died, David was heartbroken that he had broken God's law and was separated from God by sin. David and Bathsheba repented of their sin and asked for forgiveness. Then God did a work of grace in their home and gave them another child, Solomon. Solomon became the wisest man on the earth because of his pure heart early in life. Despite the sin that overtook him in later years, he was in the genealogy and lineage of Jesus Christ.

Yet Solomon's fall into sin is directly traceable to the tainted spiritual heritage he received from his adulterous parents, and to his own appetite for forbidden sexual union with hundreds of ungodly women:

*And he had seven hundred wives, princesses, and three hundred concubines: and his wives turned away his heart. For it came to pass, when Solomon was old, that **his wives turned away his heart after other gods**: and his heart was not perfect with the Lord his God, as was the heart of David his father* (1 Kings 11:3-4).

King Solomon's heart and actions were turned away from God by the 700 wives and 300 concubines he had collected to satisfy his lusts, many of them from foreign nations that worshiped demons. What a polluted house!

Again, the best advice for those who want to keep the heavens clear overhead is to "flee...youthful lusts."[11] The Bible also gives us timeless advice for handling tempting thoughts and fantasies:

> *Casting down imaginations, and every high thing that exalteth itself against the knowledge of God, and **bringing into captivity** every **thought** to the obedience of Christ* (2 Corinthians 10:5).

If you have already failed, and like the woman at the well, you want to worship God in purity once again, God's Word declares, "Whom the Son sets free is free indeed."[12] Start fresh today and restore again the joy of unblocked and unhindered prayer and communion with God.

Endnotes

1. See 2 Corinthians 2:11.
2. *Strong's,* **dabaq** (Heb., #1692).
3. *Strong's,* **join** and associated root words (Gr. #4347, #4314, and #2853.)
4. See Genesis 2:24; 1 Corinthians 6:16.
5. See Exodus 34:29-33.
6. See Genesis 2:24.
7. See Proverbs 7:23.
8. *Strong's,* **kabed** (Heb., #3516).
9. 2 Timothy 2:22a.
10. See Proverbs 6:31.
11. 2 Timothy 2:22a.
12. See John 8:36.

Chapter 5

God's Prescription
for a Breakthrough

Howbeit this kind goeth not out but by prayer and fasting
(Matthew 17:21).

Through the years, I've seen such a lack of fruit in Christendom that I have seriously wondered, "Lord, how many will make it?" I'm not so sure that everyone who is in the Body of Christ will be in the Bride of Christ! For a long time I wouldn't preach this, even though I was concerned about the people who called themselves "Christians" but lived a lifestyle that didn't match God's Word or the Lord's example. The things they were doing in their personal lives and their so-called ministries were reflecting badly on me and everyone else who named the name of Jesus. Then one day the Lord said to me when I was in prayer, "Not everyone who is in My Body will be in My Bride." That was when I realized that "the body" has an earthly connotation, but "the bride" has a heavenly connotation.

God Requires Obedience Above All Other Things
Now after years of study and of holding my peace about this, I want to give you several Scriptures, including some quotes from Jesus, that support my statement. Obedience is all-important. This is why there will be many professors, but few possessors.

To Obey Is to Do God's Will

> **Not every one** that saith unto Me, Lord, Lord, shall enter into the kingdom of heaven; but he that doeth the will of My Father which is in heaven. Many will say to Me in that day, Lord, Lord, have we not prophesied in Thy name? and in Thy name have cast out devils? and in Thy name done many wonderful works? And then will I profess unto them, I never knew you: depart from Me, ye that work iniquity (Matthew 7:21-23).

Jesus said, "Many will say to Me in that day [not a few, but many], Lord, Lord, have we not prophesied in Thy name?" Jesus wasn't talking about "lost" people. These people knew God. They had gone beyond the salvation stage where they accepted Jesus as Savior. They had progressed to the stage where they had accepted Jesus as Lord, because the Bible says that "no man can say that Jesus is the Lord, but by the Holy Ghost."[1] They were the real McCoys.

Jesus didn't say that they *tried* to cast out devils. He said that they cast out devils in His name. The Bible teaches that you can't cast out devils unless you first bind the strongman in the house.[2] These people had the power to cast out devils! Jesus sent out 70 disciples with the power to cast out devils—including Judas Iscariot! They didn't see the real issue. It isn't what you do *for* God, how many people you help, or all the good things you do. The issue is, are you under submission to Him?

If you look closely, you will see that Jesus didn't dispute the things these people were saying. He never disputed their claims that they prophesied in His name—because they did! He didn't correct them and say they had given a "false" prophecy. He didn't deny that they had done "many wonderful works" in His name. The problem is that they had not done "the will of the Father." This earned them one of the strongest rebukes in the Bible. Jesus said,

> And then will I profess unto them, I never knew you: depart from Me,
> ye that work iniquity (Matthew 7:23).

In effect, Jesus was saying, "I never approved of you, you workers of lawlessness [iniquity] who would have no law over you. You took the gift, but left the Giver. You took the anointing, but never bowed your knee to the Lord. You are like a wild maverick going off and doing your own thing."

It is safe to say that everyone who reads this book can name certain unharnessed mavericks who are out there roaming the Kingdom, doing all kinds of big things for God. The problem is that when the Lord says, "Heel!" they just turn a deaf ear and keep going headstrong in their so-called ministry. Powerful works and ministries have never been the issue. When the 70 disciples came back to Jesus and said excitedly, "Even the devils are subject to us!" Jesus said,

...I beheld Satan as lightning fall from heaven. ...rejoice not, that the spirits are subject unto you; but rather rejoice, because your names are written in heaven (Luke 10:18,20).

In other words, Jesus was saying, "Big deal. I'm not impressed that devils are subject to you. I want to see you obey My commands so you can be part of My Kingdom." The original Greek manuscripts include the word *ori* in this passage:

And then will I profess unto them, I never knew you... (Matthew 7:23).

This word was used like a quotation mark to introduce a direct quote. Jesus didn't simply say, "I never knew you." He was quoting a very special rabbinic phrase that everyone in the audience understood. Leading scholars who have studied the Jewish traditions from the Talmud and the Midrash that appear in the Greek New Testament say that "the words *'I never knew you'* were used by rabbis as a *banish formula.*"[3] This phrase had the effect and authority of a judge's final sentence declared over a disobedient defendant. Jesus is serious about obedience.

To Obey Is to Prepare for the Coming of Christ

In Matthew 25, Jesus showed us that He demands advanced preparation and foresight from those who wish to attend His wedding banquet. In the parable of the wise and foolish virgins, **all** ten women who were waiting for the Bridegroom were virgins. They **all** were asleep, they **all** had lamps, **and** they **all** woke up at the same time. The only difference between the five wise virgins and the five foolish virgins became apparent when the friend of the bridegroom suddenly woke them, saying, "Behold, the bridegroom cometh."[4] The Bible says that *all ten virgins* woke up and began to trim the wicks on their lamps. Then the five foolish virgins realized that all the oil in their lamps had already burned, and they had brought no extra oil to refill their lamps.

The five wise virgins who had purchased enough oil to last for the whole wedding refused to share their oil supply. They had purchased more oil than their lamps could hold because they had carefully counted the cost and prepared in advance by seeking a double portion from the oil seller. Thus they told the five foolish virgins: "Go get your oil at the same place we got ours!"[5] So the foolish virgins took their empty lamps into town to buy oil. While they were gone, the bridegroom came and they were shut out of the wedding feast.

This is a sobering picture of the last days. You may have a lamp, you may be a virgin, and you may awaken with all the other virgins in the Body of Christ when the Bridegroom comes, but if you have not prepared in advance as the Master has commanded, you may not be part of His wedding feast. God wants more than the right clothing, the right tools (or gifts), the right college or seminary degrees, or the right religious words. He demands obedience.

Parents want their children to obey. Hugs, kisses, and gifts can't take the place of good old-fashioned obedience. Where there is obedience, these expressions of love flow naturally between parents and children. The same is true of our relationship with God. God has fixed life so that it just won't work without Him! Obedience is the secret weapon of every Christian, great or small, young or old.

To Obey Is to Honestly Seek God and to Love as He Loves
Sometimes our love for God wanes and our relationship with Him grows cold from a lack of obedience. Revival revives that which is nearly dead or forgotten. It returns us to our first love, our fieriest passion, and our deepest convictions. It revitalizes our spirit-man, restores its rule over the soul and the flesh, and totally

reorders our priorities according to God's will. Revival reaches through a small hole in heavens of brass and clears the skies for an even mightier outpouring of God's presence.

A flood of dishonesty and hypocrisy has stolen the vigor of the Church. Many of God's people have become masqueraders who stage a parade of pretense every Sunday morning from coast to coast! They say, "We are Christ's disciples," but they don't do what He commands. This causes a great problem for God's people because God demands obedience. He talks more about obedience and disobedience than anything else in the Bible. We need a revival of honesty and holiness in our homes and churches.

Part of the problem is that we have our own ideas of what is holy and what is not. We seek the gifts of the Spirit instead of the Giver of the gifts. We confess God's Word but don't bother to seek or obey the God of the Word. We preach volumes on love but crucify anybody who dares to disagree with us. We talk holy on Sunday and walk lowly on Monday. We argue and withdraw church membership over the slightest differences of church doctrine, forgetting that true disciples are to be known not by their doctrine, but by their love for one another. We love the excitement and power of revival but are not willing to pay the price of persistently seeking the God of revival. God is sick of our facade.

Yet they seek Me daily, and delight to know My ways...they take delight in approaching to God. Wherefore have we fasted, say they, and Thou seest not? wherefore have we afflicted our soul, and Thou takest no knowledge? Behold, in the day of your fast ye find pleasure, and exact all your labours. Behold, ye fast for strife and debate, and to smite with the fist of wickedness: ye shall not fast as ye do this day, to make your voice to be heard on high. Is it such a fast that I have chosen? a day for a man to afflict his soul? is it to bow down his head as a bulrush, and to spread sackcloth and ashes under him? wilt thou call this a fast, and an acceptable day to the Lord? (Isaiah 58:2-5).

God spoke this message to His people through the prophet Isaiah. He was chastising the descendants of Abraham, the people of the ark and the Temple, because they had fallen in love with the letter of the law while neglecting the Spirit behind it. Do you realize that Jesus did the same thing in the New Testament? He directed most of His anger toward the "church-goers" of His time, not the sinners! If this is a sobering thought for you, consider the following:

**God abhors what we think He scarcely notices,
and He scarcely notices what we think He abhors.**

One time a prostitute came to our revival service wearing red hot-pants and a halter top with a bare midriff. When the Holy Spirit touched her heart during the service, she literally ran down to the altar to repent of her sin and receive forgiveness. She was gloriously saved that day, but when she went forward, I had three ladies stand discreetly behind her with prayer cloths to shield the parts of her body that were exposed to the congregation when she knelt down at the altar. I knew that certain people in the congregation at the time would be distracted or offended by the woman's appearance.

Do you think God was distracted or offended by that young woman's clothing? *Absolutely not!* He was overjoyed to see another lost soul yielding to conviction and unashamedly repenting. He wasn't the least bit embarrassed, and we shouldn't be either. Too many of us have forgotten that the Church is supposed to be a hospital for sinners, not just a museum for saints.

God is not impressed by outward appearances or clothing, but He goes out of His way to chastise hypocrisy and dishonesty in His household! These two elements are often primary ingredients in creating brassy heavens. Jesus confronted the most respected religious leaders of His age with this scathing accusation:

Woe unto you, scribes and Pharisees, hypocrites! for ye are like unto whited sepulchres, which indeed appear beautiful outward, but are within full of dead men's bones, and of all uncleanness. Even so ye also outwardly appear righteous unto men, but within ye are full of hypocrisy and iniquity (Matthew 23:27-28).

To Obey Is to Pray and to Keep God's Chosen Fast
Our problem is not the devil or demon spirits; it is *our disobedience.* There is probably less genuine prayer going up to Heaven

now than there has ever been. If prayer is rare, then true heartfelt, biblical, Spirit-led fasting is almost nonexistent in the modern Church! Too many of us take delight in approaching God because we hope to get something from Him. Then we grumble and complain if we don't get it. We even try to manipulate God with guilt and innuendo just like we manipulate one another. Likewise, when we do fast, we usually do it so that God will hear our prayers better. God doesn't have a hearing problem. We do.

God has given us certain crowbars to help us pry and jar our flesh from the seat of authority so that our spirits can resume control and the heavens can become clear. Because Jesus knew that His disciples would face many things when they continued His work of carrying the gospel to the world after He was gone, He constantly put them in situations where they had to stretch their faith and face the risk of failure. The disciples cast out demons many times, but one day they encountered a demon so powerful that it refused to obey their commands. Matthew chapter 17 describes this event when the disciples learned about two of the most powerful crowbars God gives us:

> *Then came the disciples to Jesus apart, and said, Why could not we cast him out? And Jesus said unto them, Because of your unbelief: for verily I say unto you, If ye have faith as a grain of mustard seed, ye shall say unto this mountain, Remove hence to yonder place; and it shall remove; and nothing shall be impossible unto you. Howbeit **this kind goeth not out but by prayer and fasting** (Matthew 17:19-21).*

Some bondage, yokes, bands, and even spirits will release their victims only when someone dares to fast and pray until the enemy goes away. Business as usual won't do. God's chosen prescription is fasting and praying until the powers of evil are defeated.

Spirit-led prayer and fasting is so important because it turns our eyes from ourselves, and our own cloudy skies, toward those things that are on the heart of God. In Isaiah's day, the Jewish religious leaders had perfected the art of the fast as a religious exercise. Although they prayed faithfully to God every day, it was only an act. They fasted and prayed with wrong motives. From beginning to end, their eyes were on themselves and those things that pleased men the most. Therefore, their prayer and fasting yielded no fruit to demonstrate that they had been changed through a real encounter with God.

So disturbed was God by this behavior that He did something drastic that seemed to be out of order when compared with the instructions He had given to Moses about priestly service and worship. He made it clear to the Jewish leaders that God scarcely notices what men think He abhors. God demanded that men observe a new kind of fast:

> *Is not this the fast that I have chosen? to loose the bands of wickedness, to undo the heavy burdens, and to let the oppressed go free, and that ye break every yoke? Is it not to deal thy bread to the hungry, and that thou bring the poor that are cast out to thy house? when thou seest the naked, that thou cover him; and that thou hide not thyself from thine own flesh?* (Isaiah 58:6-7).

The Fast (Life) That Pleases God

These verses list seven key characteristics of the kind of fast (and the kind of life) that pleases God. They are God's prescription for breaking through the brassiest of heavens. He calls us to:

1. *Loose the bands of wickedness and undo the heavy burdens.*
2. *Let the oppressed go free.*
3. *Break every yoke.*
4. *Deal thy bread to the hungry.*
5. *Bring the poor that are cast out into thy house.*
6. *Cover the naked.*
7. *Do not hide thyself from thine own flesh.*

Every one of these points demands that we add works to our faith. It isn't enough to have faith. Our faith, if it is genuine, must show practical fruit in our personal actions toward others. If the fruit is missing, we must ask ourselves if our faith is genuine. Thus, if the Church is isolated and out of touch with the needs of people today, it is probably because you and I are isolated and out of touch. Our faith isn't having an impact where we live.

Jesus Christ is again sending His Church into the world with the good news of the gospel. God's requirement for us to share in the work is that we must pray, fast, and forsake our private religion and our exclusive salvation by isolation. We have good news! Now we must share it with those who need it!

1. *Loose the bands of wickedness and undo the heavy burdens.*

According to *Merriam-Webster's Collegiate Dictionary*, a *band* is "something that confines or constricts while allowing a degree of movement; something that binds or restrains legally, morally, or spiritually." The word can also be used to mean "a group of persons, animals, or things."[6]

Heavy burdens and bands of wickedness may refer to the unlawful restraint and control imposed on vulnerable people by the ungodly men and systems of this world. These men and their systems may be inspired and guided by satan's hand, but the truth remains that the hand of man is the instrument inflicting this pain and hardship on innocent people. God has called us to loosen these bands and to undo the heavy burdens God never intended men to carry. Some of the worst bands and burdens are rooted in the religious hypocrisy of men.

Jesus referred to these heavy burdens when He taught His disciples:

All therefore whatsoever they bid you observe, that observe and do; but do not ye after their works: for they say, and do not. For they bind heavy burdens and grievous to be borne, and lay them on men's shoulders; but they themselves will not move them with one of their fingers (Matthew 23:3-4).

The most common band of wickedness at work in the world is the false religious idea that we have to be cleaned up and holy before we can come to God. Self-righteous Christians have fostered this lie for centuries, a lie that has kept countless millions out of God's Kingdom. This band of wickedness has to be loosened and destroyed by the truth that God calls as many as will come to cling to the cross, repenting of their sin and receiving forgiveness. Jesus said it best:

...They that are whole have no need of the physician, but they that are sick: I came not to call the righteous, but sinners to repentance (Mark 2:17).

Bands in the Church

Some churches have a degree of movement that allows them to advance only to a certain point in praise or prayer. They can't go any further. In some cases, a band of disobedience or of man-made religious tradition is holding them back. God wants us to release our cherished sins, our prejudices, and our preconceived ideas about how He works so that He can take us farther in His glory. If we dare to leap into the river of His Spirit with all our hearts, we won't have to live the rest of our days in frustration, mourning over a haunting void in our spiritual lives.

Even more common are the bands that bind us to some darkness that still haunts us from long before we came to Christ. These bands keep us from moving on in our walk with Jesus because they prevent us from believing that anything will ever change. This is when the support and encouragement of God's people can especially make a difference. The Word tells us to bear one another's burdens,[7] and to rejoice with those who rejoice, and weep with those who weep.[8] This is what the Body of Christ is all about.

The enemy also brings bands of affliction against individuals and families in the Church whom he has targeted for destruction. Any time we see a brother or sister under attack from the enemy, we shouldn't hesitate to jump in and bring assistance through prayer, command, or deed. If our brother is battling with a recurring sin or temptation, for example, we can encourage him to redirect his thoughts to the good things God has already done for him, to listen to worship tapes, and to read a book that will strengthen his faith. We can also be sure that we are ready to stand with him when he falls, even if he falls again and again. Believers facing these kinds of problems need special support and care until they can renew their minds in the Word of God and overcome the past, or whatever present circumstance, relationship, or experience is causing them to stumble. In this way, even the most stubborn bands that inhibit the growth of believers—including alcohol, drugs, pornography, eating disorders, homosexuality, and a host of other traps to which man is vulnerable—can be broken.

Bands in the World

John the apostle said that the whole world lies "in wickedness."[9] Jesus said,

Ye are the light of the world. A city that is set on an hill cannot be hid (Matthew 5:14).

Ye are the salt of the earth: but if the salt have lost his savour, wherewith shall it be salted? it is thenceforth good for nothing, but to be cast out, and to be trodden under foot of men (Matthew 5:13).

God does not intend for His people to remain neutral or invisible. He put us in this world to invade, disturb, and occupy with authority everything that satan has stolen. But our salt isn't salty, our light isn't lit, and the city of God has been hidden by respectability and compromise. We have so blended into the world with ungodly ease that the transforming power of God is too often weakened or completely absent. Revival will change this.

Jesus constantly put His followers on the front line of ministry to disciple them. He is doing the same thing today with the Church. He wants to send us out to cities and towns with the gospel, just like He sent out the 70 in Luke 10:1. His last words before ascending to the Father were words of commission, delegation, and assignment:

Go ye therefore, and teach all nations, baptizing them in the name of the Father, and of the Son, and of the Holy Ghost: teaching them to observe all things whatsoever I have commanded you: and, lo, I am with you alway, even unto the end of the world. Amen (Matthew 28:19-20).

He described those who enter into His new covenant in dynamic terms that can only be understood as supernatural:

And these signs shall follow them that believe; In My name shall they cast out devils; they shall speak with new tongues; they shall take up serpents; and if they drink any deadly thing, it shall not hurt them; they shall lay hands on the sick, and they shall recover (Mark 16:17-18).

These people of God know how to loosen bands of wickedness and undo heavy burdens. They are actively doing His work in the world. Unfortunately, the modern Church often groups these uncomfortable passages with other Bible verses that are lumped under the phrase, "They passed away with the apostles."

Obviously, the apostles functioned in the kind of power these passages describe. Throughout the New Testament we see that they aggressively assaulted the kingdom of darkness everywhere they went. They removed the heavy burdens of pharisaic legalism from Jewish believers and untied the weight of darkness that clung to Gentile converts. Others who shared the work of the gospel also served in this power. Stephen was a deacon, a table waiter who worked great miracles among the sick. John Mark, a young disciple who outlived Paul, and perhaps all the rest of the apostles, also ministered with authority.

Throughout Church history, men and women have risen up in the power of the Lord to bring deliverance and freedom from the bands of wickedness. The Church of today can no longer ignore the command to loosen the bands of wickedness and undo heavy burdens. To do so is to forsake the very lifework of the Church. To be sure, we cannot accomplish this work apart from the *power* of the Holy Ghost, but accomplish it we must!

2. *Let the oppressed go free.*
    The Bible says,
    > *...God anointed Jesus of Nazareth with the Holy Ghost and with power: who went about doing good, and healing all that were oppressed of the devil; for God was with Him* (Acts 10:38).

The Greek word for oppression is *katadunasteuo*, which means "to exercise dominion against."[10] The Hebrew word used in Isaiah 58:6 for "oppressed" is *ratsats*, which means "to crack in pieces, to break, bruise, crush, discourage, oppress, struggle together."[11]

Our planet is being oppressed and bruised by a cruel taskmaster. The Church should be the one bright hope that promises the world freedom. After all, we represent the living Christ. But where are we? Where is the evidence that we are releasing the oppressed from the many afflictions that enslave them? Freedom for the downtrodden will not become reality until the Church wakes up and begins to emancipate these people in the name of Jesus Christ! Freedom won't come through a new president, a psychologist's couch, or a new batch of government programs. The only way a tyrant's authority can be removed is for a more powerful ruler to force him from his throne. The oppressed will see the dominion of the enemy cast down only when the Church rises up in the authority of Jesus Christ, the King of kings and Lord of lords.

Most of the prayers we offer in church services and in our homes are for ourselves. This cannot continue. The whole point of Isaiah 58 is to compel God's people to turn their eyes and desires away from themselves to the needs of oppressed, hurting people. God wants us to get alone with Him, praying and fasting for the lost. If we do, He will give us the faith and power to break every band and to loose those who are bound. He will send us more business than we can possibly take care of.

3. Break every yoke.

A yoke was a sign of absolute slavery and captivity in the ancient world. Yokes were reserved for heavy work animals such as oxen and donkeys. They were also used as vindictive instruments to further humiliate despised, defeated, enslaved prisoners. When the Philistines wanted to totally humiliate their most hated enemy, they put a yoke on Samson and made him grind corn, doing the work of an ox.

A yoke also represented a future of perpetual captivity and soul-searing subjection. The only way to free a person from a yoke of bondage was to break it into pieces, since yokes were attached permanently. They chaffed the neck and rubbed lasting sores on their victims day and night. Often a person who was bound by a yoke was unable to reach even his own head to relieve an itch, remove something from his eye, or feed himself. The yoke rendered him helpless.

This world has functioned under thickened skies for so long that millions of people live in perpetual darkness under the yoke of demonic bondage. Although the Church has been given the keys to hell, death, and the grave, we have failed to effectively exercise this power. What a shame it will be if we fail to rouse ourselves from sleep and snap the yokes of the helpless in Jesus' name! My friend, God will hold us responsible for every act of love, kindness, and redemption that we choose *not* to do because we love comfort and ease.

4. *Deal thy bread to the hungry.*

The Jews of Isaiah's day were overly concerned with formulating purely spiritual interpretations of the Scriptures. It seemed that the longer and more religiously they fasted, the more unjust their treatment of those people who were outside their religious inner circle became. They disdained the poor and considered poverty to be proof of a man's wickedness and sin, an attitude erroneously held by many Christians today.

The Church has grown accustomed to letting soup kitchens and relief agencies feed the hungry. Once a year we send double-digit checks off to national and international organizations to feed the poor "over there." We may even drop a can or two in the local food bank box that is hidden behind the coatrack out back. In essence, our attitudes say, "We've done our good deed. Now what's for dinner, Pastor? Preach to us."

I think we need to read the Book again. The Bible says of the fast God has chosen,

Is it not to deal thy [your] *bread to the hungry...?* (Isaiah 58:7a)

God wants our charity and sharing to be personal and up close. He wants us to look into the eyes of the hungry and share from our abundance—or even from our need.

There is something about hands-on ministry and sharing that transforms the heart and the soul. There is something about rubbing shoulders with the hungry, the lost, and the wounded that keeps our eyes on Jesus Christ and our egos on the ground, where they belong. God planned it this way because He knows that when we personally share our bread with another person, we also share love, encouragement, and the reassurance that the person we serve is valuable and precious in the sight of both God and man. This is valuable and rare indeed. Our religion becomes a lifestyle of Christlike sharing, loving, and redeeming. After all, if Jesus were to walk among us today, where would we find Him—with the satisfied or the hungry?

This may not sound like a revival message, but it is. The quickest way to doom a revival or a move of God is to keep it within the four walls of a church building. Many of us here at Brownsville pray fervently that God will use us to move this revival beyond our four walls and into our neighborhoods and the city at large. True revival invades every area of life, especially those parts where there is pain.

5. *Bring the poor that are cast out into thy house.*

Perhaps you didn't notice it, but Isaiah used that irritating word "thy [your]" again. Many Christians struggle with the implications of this word. They fall into the error of asking questions such as, "God, what am I supposed to do? Should I go downtown and pick up a drifter?" The answer is simple: Follow the leading of the Holy Spirit. The Scriptures say,

> *The steps of a good man are ordered by the Lord: and He delighteth in his way* (Psalm 37:23).

We know this to be true, but we don't act like it.

Obviously the wisdom of God is needed any time you consider bringing a stranger into your home, but most of the time you won't be dealing with strangers. A church in revival is a growing church that touches thousands of lives each month. These people always include families who are dealing with the loss of income due to layoffs, sickness, desertion, or the untimely death of a breadwinner. Often they struggle through each week without a husband or father to carry the financial load. A church that is seriously caring for the poor and hungry will learn to recognize and respond to these needs. Like Jesus, they will reach out to meet not only spiritual needs but also the physical needs that sharing food and housing can help to satisfy. They will learn to trust God to help them fulfill all the needs of the hurting people He brings into their midst.

The dividends of sharing our bounty and shelter with others are immeasurable. Families who make it a practice to open their homes to those who are facing real crises consistently demonstrate a deeper joy and vibrancy in their walk with God. They witness the miraculous on a day-to-day basis as they share with their guests until God, by His grace, take these needy ones from deep need to total supply. Empty religion has no chance when the miraculous provision of God and the genuine love of Christ are on the scene.

6. *Cover the naked.*

In the words, "...when thou seest the naked, that thou cover him,"[12] God is again removing this job from the hands of formal institutionalized systems and plopping it right into our laps. The response He speaks of is almost impulsive and instant. There is no time to premeditate!

The naked can be many people, including those who are exposed to the elements and eyes of the world, and those who are damaged by the words of accusers or the criticism of the self-righteous. Anytime you see someone who needs clothing or covering, be quick to act on his behalf.

Be quick also to cover believers who have fallen into sin and have repented. The Bible says,

Hatred stirreth up strifes: but love covereth all sins (Proverbs 10:12).

We are too quick to call for a lynch party when someone in our churches falls into sin. If there is genuine repentance, we need to move quickly to hide his nakedness with love and encouragement. God never said that we wouldn't fail in this life. He did say,

For a just man falleth seven times, and riseth up again (Proverbs 24:16a).

7. *Do not hide thyself from thine own flesh.*

Have you ever heard someone say, "Well, you can pick your friends, but you're stuck with family"? This homespun proverb explains why so many people are guilty of hiding from the members of their own families. It also explains why so many people refuse to commit and submit to a local family of believers. We don't have the option to pick and choose our own family members. Neither is God asking for our opinion.

Too many Christians have accepted the wander and roam plan of the world, casting off all obligations to family members, as well as the local church. This is quite dangerous, since family life and church life are paramount in God's plan. This is true because the character of God is best formed in the heat and pressure of long-term, mandatory fellowship with other people who may or may not agree with you on every detail. More character growth and learning takes place in the crucible of family life than in any other area of human existence. When you can't escape from someone's company, you are forced to learn how to get along with him.

The family is God's safety net for a lifetime. Modern society, in its wisdom, has tried to dismantle the family. However, the family structure has worked for thousands of years in every culture on earth. Long before there were welfare agencies, government assistance programs, and Social Security, there was family. The family not only provided for the physical necessities of its members but also policed those among them who were not diligent about seeking work or meeting their responsibilities. This is virtually impossible for monolithic government agencies. Even the Church has fallen into the "let the government do it" mentality.

Personal responsibility and duty were once at the heart of all family relationships. Children knew that they had an inherent responsibility to care for their parents in old age, just as their parents had cared for them in infancy. The sick, the disabled, and failing were never abandoned. They were enfolded and carried as long as was necessary. After all, they were family. Where personal responsibility and duty are discarded, the family safety net fails. It is time for the Church to restore God's standard of responsibility to every

Christian home and congregation. Paul made this rule of the New Covenant clear:

> *But if any provide not for his own, and specially for those of his own house, he hath denied the faith, and is worse than an infidel* (1 Timothy 5:8).

One reason the Jews have prospered in virtually every country and culture in which they have located is that they tend to take care of family. If a man settles in a new city and establishes a business there, family members generally work in the business and help it to become stable.

When the man's son or nephew reaches manhood, the business owner is expected to train the young man in the family business and either offer him a position there or help him to establish a new business in a new area. Profits tend to be funneled right back into family businesses and the local Jewish community. Likewise, if a family member gets in trouble or needs someone to speak for him in a time of need, the family is there. If a father dies leaving a widow and children, the family supports them financially, and later trains the children or places them in productive jobs. Most loans are made within the community, and few, if any, people ever default on these family loans.

> *Two are better than one; because they have a good reward for their labour. For if they fall, the one will lift up his fellow: but woe to him that is alone when he falleth; for he hath not another to help him up. Again, if two lie together, then they have heat: but how can one be warm alone? And if one prevail against him, two shall withstand him; and **a threefold cord is not quickly broken*** (Ecclesiastes 4:9-12).

God established the family and the Church for good reasons. The union of Christ, the family, and the Church forms a threefold cord upon which we can safely build our lives and effectively minister to the hurting. True revival produces the chosen fast of God in His Church and takes the river of God and His practical provisions into every street and byway.

Endnotes

1. 1 Corinthians 12:3.
2. Matthew 12:29.
3. H.L. Strack and P. Billerbeck, *Kommentar zum Neuen Testament aus Talmust end Midrasch*, 6 vols. (Munich: C.H. Beck, 1965) in Fritz Reinecker and Cleon Rogers, *A Linguistic Key to the Greek New Testament* (Grand Rapids, MI: The Zondervan Corporation, 1976, 1980), pp. 21-22.
4. Matthew 25:6.
5. See Matthew 25:9.
6. *Merriam-Webster's Collegiate Dictionary*, 10th ed. (Springfield, MA: Merriam-Webster, Inc., 1994), p. 89.
7. See Galatians 6:2.
8. See Romans 12:15.
9. 1 John 5:19.
10. *Strong's*, **oppressed**, (Gr., #2616).
11. *Strong's*, (Heb., #7533).
12. Isaiah 58:7b.

Chapter 6

Is There Leprosy in Your House?

God has a dream for your home. He wants your house to be a haven. He's planned that your family and your guests will be contented when you sit down for fellowship. He intends that your dwelling place will be a productive and fertile garden where His Spirit reigns and you are free to speak of His Word and His anointing. Your home, as God has prescribed it should be, is a place filled with a rich atmosphere of love and acceptance. Words of revelation knowledge fall frequently from your lips, and you speak freely about the fire of revival and the moving of God's Spirit.

In this holy house dedicated to God and sealed in peace, the Holy Spirit speaks directly to your heart with anointed *rhema* words, helping you to win souls and to free the hurting in your neighborhood or workplace. The divine Teacher is welcomed as He makes the Word of God come alive in your heart, burning its truth deeply into your spirit. Even while you sleep, the Comforter comes over you with divine creativity and direction, ordering your steps for the day ahead. God is pleased to dwell in this house. He finds great joy in the love and fellowship.

Does Your Home Match God's Dream?

Not all homes match this picture. If we are honest, few of us would say that God's dream is lived out in our houses. How would you describe your house? Do you barely shut the door of your car or your home following the church service, before all hell breaks loose? Are you and your spouse constantly fighting? Are temper tantrums and fits of rage commonplace? Do you regularly fill your children's ears with cutting words, negative comments, and belittling sarcasm? Does bickering over unimportant details you can't even remember later fill the rooms of your house? Is verbal battering and emotional abuse so prevalent that your family avoids sharing meals together?

If you answered yes to one or more of these questions, something is seriously wrong with your home. You can't ignore this problem, my friend, consoling yourself with the knowledge that other people live the same way. Dismissing a problem is never the answer, but first you must admit that you have a problem, that a plague is loose in your house, trying to destroy you and your family.

When revival broke out, I noticed that people who had been touched by the power of God would get up off the floor and go home rejoicing. Sometimes entire families—father, mother, children, grandparents—lay on the floor for hours under the power of God. But on the way home, they ended up in a big fight! Children who had shed tears under the anointing of God became rude, disobedient boys and girls who openly challenged their parents and one another.

My heart ached as I heard one story after another from people who were just wonderful in church but just awful in their homes. When they left the environment of worship and of surrender to God and entered their homes, the home environment produced a quite disturbing change in them. They behaved differently because their homes were polluted and contaminated by things that created a significantly different atmosphere than that at church.

God Will Not Live With the Devil or His Stuff

As a pastor, I am interested in long-term fruits that can be seen. Genuine revival should bring renewal and refreshing into every area of our lives, no matter where we are. Change that is evident only the few hours a week we spend in a revival meeting has little or no value. So I began to intercede for these families that changed so drastically once they entered their home environment. I beseeched the Lord to show me the root and the cure for this prevalent problem. One day the Lord said to me,

If My people don't get rid of the unclean things in their homes and lives, My precious Spirit and glory will not stay in the church very long. I have come to give them the strength to cast out the unclean things.

The Lord showed me that the holy gifts and anointing these folks received from Him in the church services weren't sticking because they didn't take them home with them. God's presence was clashing with the climate of their homes. God is reviving us to give us the strength and resolve to rise up and rid our homes of the unclean things that vex them.

Holiness has been a characteristic of this revival because it is a characteristic of God. Since He answered our prayers for a visitation of His presence, the poverty of our holiness is evident in every service. Even the most mature and holy among us still sense an urgent need to repent before God and to be cleansed anew by His river, the Holy Spirit.

This need to repent does not stop once we leave the church building. God requires holiness in all aspects of our lives. He has come to touch us, help us, sanctify us, and fix us, but He will not bless us when we sin. We cannot expect the Lord's presence to stay with us if we go home from church to a house tainted by pornography, R-rated TV shows, and other willful sin. In truth, we would be truly dismayed should the Lord choose to enter such a home, for the joy we find in God's presence would soon be exchanged for weeping. While the sudden appearance of God to a holy people brings unspeakable joy, the same appearing in an unclean congregation or household brings devastation and destruction.

God will not live with sin. If we choose to forsake the Lord, re-turning to our old ways and despising the blessings of His revival fire, we are fools. Then God's presence works against us, since He requires that we repent and live holy lives, even as He is holy.

Since Father's Day of 1995, more than 100,000 souls have come to the altars in Pensacola to be born again by the Spirit of God. This isn't a man-made revival. It was initiated by God alone. He has moved upon our hearts, giving us a tremendous spirit of re-pentance and holiness. He hungers for this spirit to permeate our homes, giving us the will to get our houses in order.

Those who refuse to take God's overcoming anointing home show by their lack of obedience that they have spurned the work of God in their lives. They have chosen to return to the sin that they had repented of. How difficult will be their path!

For it had been better for them not to have known the way of righteous-ness, than, after they have known it, to turn from the holy command-ment delivered unto them. But it is happened unto them according to the true proverb, The dog is turned to his own vomit again; and the sow that was washed to her wallowing in the mire (2 Peter 2:21-22).

God is omniscient. He cannot be fooled, for He sees all things. He knows exactly what you are thinking at this very moment, and He sees those things that you keep hidden because you are ashamed of them. He sees and remembers what goes on behind the closed doors of your office and your home. He can describe in detail the title and contents of every videotape cassette that is stacked near your VCR, as well as those "special videos" you've hid-den from the kids or the preacher. He hears your words, the times you misuse His name or speak to your spouse, your parents, or your children with disrespect. He hears your phone conversations and watches you read your mail.

Sin Makes a House Barren or Sterile

God gave me a solemn warning that the anointing and power of this revival will lift if His people don't go into their homes and have a Holy Ghost housecleaning. Our holy God will not condone or contribute to a double standard of holiness in the Church and sinfulness in our homes. One of the telltale signs of a spiritually troubled home is what I call sterility. This sterility or barrenness makes your home an unsuitable place to pray. Indeed, you may find that it is difficult or unenjoyable to pray at home. A brooding heaviness permeates the air, and attitudes and moods are often quite volatile. (This same sterility can affect local congregations. A troubled church will often have a stifling environment that seems to wither its members and everything connected with it.)

Children die quickly in a sterile or barren environment. Being very sensitive to the spirit realm, they need the covering and protection of their parents to ward off spiritual assaults. When parents go wrong, vulnerable children suffer. Some children I've ministered to were withered at home because their fathers were very harsh, raging and cursing at their children. Others bore the effects of parental conflict because one parent had turned on the other. Still other children sustained spiritual damage because their fathers were constantly cursing and criticizing their wives, saying things like, "You're no good. You don't even take care of me. Just look at the sorry state of this house. It's a pigpen!" This constant stream of negative words hurt not only the women but also the children in the home.

Negative words and deeds are always destructive. Like a hot desert wind scorches and withers all living things in its path, the hot breath of criticism and cutting words withers the lives of all who are in the home, producing sterility and eventual death. Because the spirits of children are particularly susceptible to negative words and deeds, they suffer whether the negative, damning words are spoken directly to them or to another person in the house.

Each of us must honestly ask himself, "Is there fertility or sterility in my home? Are the people under my roof budding, thriving, and appropriately maturing, or has their growth been stunted by withering words and deeds?" Sometimes we have difficulty giving an honest appraisal of our homes. Then it is time to do some careful evaluation, intentionally observing how family members respond to us and to other members of the family. For example, are your spouse and your children afraid of you? Do they tense up when you walk by? Are you unpredictable or strange in your ways, responding one way today and another way tomorrow, with little or no pattern to your responses? Do you have a chronically bad attitude? Are the people living with you always trying to figure out whether you are in a good mood or a bad mood, so they can alter their words and behavior accordingly? Some kids can't wait to turn 18 so they can leave that sterile, dry, and oppressed place called home.

My friend, you have serious problems in your house if happiness, joy, vitality, and life are absent. Whatever measure of love, joy, peace, and contentment you see in the faces of your kids and your spouse is the same measure of freedom the Holy Ghost enjoys in your house!

I know that this honest evaluation of ourselves and our homes can, at times, be quite disconcerting; but don't despair. God's Word offers a cure for what plagues us. God knows exactly what problems fill your house, and He has already provided both the diagnosis and the cure.

Help for a Sterile Home

First let us diagnose the cause of the spiritual sterility in our homes. The Book of Leviticus sets forth a detailed procedure of how we should do this.

Tell the Priest: "There Is a Plague in My House!"

And the Lord spake unto Moses and unto Aaron, saying, When ye be come into the land of Canaan, which I give to you for a possession, and I put the plague of leprosy in a house of the land of your possession; and he that owneth the house shall come and tell the priest, saying, It seemeth to me there is as it were a plague in the house (Leviticus 14:33-35).

Examine the House

Then the priest shall command that they empty the house, before the priest go into it to see the plague, that all that is in the house be not made unclean: and afterward the priest shall go in to see the house:

*And he shall look on the plague, and, behold, if the plague be in the walls of the house with **hollow streaks, greenish or reddish,** which in sight are lower than the wall; then the priest shall go out of the house to the door of the house, and shut up the house seven days* (Leviticus 14:36-38).

Cleanse the House

And the priest shall come again the seventh day, and shall look: and, behold, if the plague be spread in the walls of the house; then the priest shall command that they take away the stones in which the plague is, and they shall cast them into an unclean place without the city: and he shall cause the house to be scraped within round about, and they shall pour out the dust that they scrape off without the city into an unclean place: and they shall take other stones, and put them in the place of those stones; and he shall take other mortar, and shall plaster the house (Leviticus 14:39-42).

If the House Is Still Unclean, Don't Ignore the Symptoms

And if the plague come again, and break out in the house, after that he hath taken away the stones, and after he hath scraped the house, and after it is plastered; then the priest shall come and look, and, behold, if the plague be spread in the house, it is a fretting [angry] *leprosy in the house: it is unclean. And he shall break down the house, the stones of it, and the timber thereof, and all the mortar of the house; and he shall carry them forth out of the city into an unclean place* (Leviticus 14:43-45).

Personal Cleansing and Declaring the Cure

Moreover he that goeth into the house all the while that it is shut up shall be unclean until the even. And he that lieth in the house shall wash his clothes; and he that eateth in the house shall wash his clothes. And if the priest shall come in, and look upon it, and, behold, the plague hath not spread in the house, after the house was plastered: then the priest shall pronounce the house clean, because the plague is healed (Leviticus 14:46-48).

Atonement for the House

And he shall take to cleanse the house two birds, and cedar wood, and scarlet, and hyssop: and he shall kill the one of the birds in an earthen vessel over running water: and he shall take the cedar wood, and the hyssop, and the scarlet, and the living bird, and dip them in the blood of the slain bird, and in the running water, and sprinkle the house *seven times: and he shall cleanse the house with the blood of the bird, and with the running water, and with the living bird, and with the cedar wood, and with the hyssop, and with the scarlet: but he shall let go the living bird out of the city into the open fields, and make an **atonement for the house**: and it shall be clean. This is the law for all manner of plague of leprosy, and scall* (Leviticus 14:49-54).

Leviticus is one of the first five books of the Bible, what we call the Pentateuch. These books were all written by Moses, who received them from God. Leviticus, in particular, deals with the Levitical law that God prescribed while the children of Israel were still wandering in the wilderness. These spiritual and physical housecleaning instructions were given to Moses before God's people entered Canaan. While this promised land would be a wonderful home with many blessings, God also established some precautions that His people needed to follow.

1. Tell the Priest: "There Is a Plague in My House!"

God promised His people an exceedingly good land that flowed with milk and honey. He said that He would give them houses they didn't build, wells they didn't dig, and vineyards they didn't plant.[1] However, all these blessings came with a warning: Be careful what house you move into.

Specifically, God told His people to examine the walls of their houses, whether they built their own homes or moved into houses that others had built. He wanted them to pay close attention to the walls of their dwellings. If they felt that there was a scall or leprosy there—indeed, if they sensed anything unusual in the walls of their homes—God's people were to go to the priest immediately and tell him, "I think there is a plague in my house!"

The Bible says that God is the one who put the plague of leprosy on these houses. Now why would He do that? He used the plague of leprosy as a litmus test to reveal the hidden presence of evil spirits in these Canaanite houses and building sites! Any chemist or medical lab worker will know immediately what you are talking about. They would think of the dyes, specimen stains, and chemicals that are used in medical tests. In fact, many, if not most, of the major tests performed in medical laboratories uses dyes, tinctures, and chemical reagents to reveal what is hidden from the naked eye. God used the plague of leprosy described in Leviticus chapter 14 to reveal what could not be observed with the physical eye.

2. Examine the House

Should a man find leprosy in his walls and run to tell the priest, the priest was basically to drop everything, including his usual duties in the tabernacle, and respond to this man's need. The leprosy test took a pretty high priority.

What the priests were to look for sounds pretty strange. The Bible says that the priests were to tell the occupants of the house to remove everything so that the priests could inspect every inch of the house's walls, floors, and foundation. If green or red streaks were found, the priest was to close up the house and set it under quarantine for seven days. Then he was to inspect it again. If the streaks had spread, the priest and the homeowners were to follow God's instructions without delay.

3. Cleanse the House

If the plague had spread, the family who had lived in the house had some serious housecleaning to do. This was not the "scrub with cleanser until the stains are gone" kind of cleaning. It required a major effort that included removing every contaminated stone from the walls, floors, and foundations of the dwelling. Not only the contaminants in plain view were to be removed but also those that were hidden. Thus the walls and floors had to be taken apart stone by stone so the priest could find all infected particles. Even the dust from the mortar that was chiseled out from between the stones had to be scraped off just in case the mortar also contained the plague. When all contaminated stones and mortar, including the dust, had been removed, they were to be carted to an unclean place far from the house or city and dumped there. Only then could the homeowners begin to replace the impure materials with fresh stones and mortar. When the rebuilding was complete, the priest was to close up the house for another seven days to see if the leprosy had been completely removed.

4.   If the House Is Still Unclean, Don't Ignore the Symptoms

In some cases, the priests would return to the freshly cleaned and rebuilt house after seven days and find red and green streaks running along the walls again. Even after all the trouble of inspecting the walls, the floors, and the foundation of the dwelling, and of removing and replacing stones and mortar, evidence of the leprosy would still be found. In those cases, the priests were to warn the family not to sleep, eat, or even sit in the house because it would make them unclean. They had to vacate the dwelling by nightfall because a "fretting" or "angry" leprosy had been found there.

Many people think that the Bible is referring to haunted houses when it talks about houses with leprosy. My friend, there is no such thing as a house haunted by disembodied human spirits. When a person dies, he doesn't move into a house on earth as an invisible occupant. His spirit either moves into Heaven with God or into hell with satan. Yes, I do believe that demons can oppress a house. If you don't believe me, just sign up for one of those pornographic cable channels, start watching it late at night, and see how quickly some demons move into your home!

Although finding the evidence of fretting leprosy in a house did not mean that demons were active there, it did reveal the presence of devilish contamination. Thus the seven-day test after cleansing the house was God's divine litmus test to find such impurities. Keep in mind that God is omnipotent (all-powerful), omnipresent (existing in all places at all times), and omniscient (seeing and knowing all things). He cannot be surprised or caught off guard by anyone or anything. If fretting leprosy was found in a house, He had brought it there for a reason. That reason is of vital importance for *you* today! God is never surprised!

God told Moses about this plague of leprosy long before the Jews reached Canaan because He wanted to make a point: "Moses, if the priests walk into a house and find this plague of leprosy, be very careful to dismantle the entire house immediately, block by block and timber by timber. Tear it all the way down to the ground if you have to, since deadly pollution is hidden in that house. My people must be careful to do this or they will suffer because of the corruption."

The ancient Jewish rabbis taught that God devised this plague because of the delay caused by Israel's sin at the Jordan River when they gave in to fear, doubt, and unbelief and refused to enter the Promised Land. Their sin transformed what was to have been a 40-day trip across the desert into a 40-year trek of death for that entire generation. By the time the new generation stepped onto the soil of Canaan, the news of Israel's powerful God had reached the Canaanites. They knew well the stories of Jehovah, the Hebrew God, and not surprisingly were fearful, wondering how they would keep these unstoppable invaders with the powerful God from overrunning their land. Throughout those 40 years of fretting and stewing as the Canaanite people told and retold the stories of the drowning of Pharaoh's army in the Red Sea, they looked for ways to protect themselves and to defend their property. Finally they began to say, "If that God is going to bring those Hebrews into our land, if He is going to give them our houses, our wells, our vineyards, and our land of milk and honey, we are going to hide our riches so that they have a hard time finding them."

Thus according to the rabbis, the Canaanites began to hoard their silver and gold in ingenious ways. Sometimes they devised elaborate schemes to hide it, hoping that the Jews would ultimately leave so they could retrieve their riches. At other times, they chose to convert the wealth of their jewelry into small particles so that their treasures were not readily available to the invaders.

As the years of desert wandering continued for the Israelites, the Canaanites and the Amorites melted down more and more of their silver and gold and made little demon gods or idols that were easily hid in the walls and foundations of their homes. Therefore when Israel finally entered the land of Canaan, they moved into homes that were cursed by the presence of demonic idols that had been created by the peoples who had preceded them in the land.

God devised the plague of leprosy to warn His people of the existence of these pagan idols. Many times when the Israelites pulled down the walls and dug up the floors of their homes after the telltale sign of red and green streaks had appeared, they found these small demon gods of gold and silver hidden in secret compartments throughout the dwelling. God knew all along that these idols were there. He used the plague of leprosy to share this information with His people. Why didn't God just ignore the presence of these idols? It's for the same reason He can't ignore the sin in your house. He will not co-exist with evil.

5. *Personal Cleansing and Declaring the Cure*

Many Christian homes, due to ignorance, have become houses of worship for demon gods. God has provided the sacrifice of Jesus Christ to atone for our sins, and His blood cleanses and protects all who accept Him as Savior, but He will not live in our homes if He must share them with demon gods. Many Christians, due to ignorance, expect Him to do just that. They have given room to other gods without intending to do so and now suffer the effects of this contamination. This often happens as Christians return from travels around the world, or from shopping at various international import stores, carrying demons in their shopping bags.

Call me a narrow-minded, superstitious preacher if you want to, but God's Word clearly states that He will not share a house or a room with your household gods. You are flirting with fire when you decorate your home with any number of foreign gods, including but not limited to the following:

1. Voodoo dolls and amulets from the Caribbean;
2. Scarabs, figurines, Hindu idols, charms, and Chinese joss from the Middle and Far East;
3. Fetishes, talismans, ritual drums, witch doctor charms, and medicine dolls from Africa;

4. Hawaiian "tiki" gods, kachina dolls (from ancient Hopi/ Pueblo Indians), potlatch figurines, good luck charms, and even divining rods of witch hazel from the United States;
5. Animist figures and art from the shamanists of Mexico.

These things were created and named for the worship and veneration of evil spirits, not God. Even it you say, "Well, I certainly don't worship them," you still owe God an explanation of why you openly display them in the rooms of your house. That was the custom of Canaan, a practice that still dominates many religions around the world. I'm telling you, God will not play house with devils or the stuff of devils. Neither will He continue to grace your home if you refuse to clean out the rest of the filth that contaminates it.

You can go into a revival service, fall on the floor, and shake like a leaf in an autumn wind, but I'll say, "So what?" if you go right back home and live the same kind of sinful life that God has warned you about for the past five years. Who are you trying to fool? No matter how much you run, dance, or shake, or how many glowing testimonies you give about the glorious visitation of God you experienced, don't try to tell me that the anointing of God is in your house if you continue to treat your spouse like dirt; to fall asleep in front of questionable movies that you tuned in to on Showtime, Cinemax, HBO, or the Playboy channel; or to page through magazines, look at videos, or read books that contain ungodly contents. Likewise, don't play holy in the church house if you still abuse your spouse or children with temper tantrums, scathing accusations, or ungodly language.

Many people want to be in church because they like the peace and comfort of God's presence. They say, "This is so wonderful. I feel the presence of God here." God is not content that you should experience His presence only when you come to church. He wants you to take His nearness and His holiness home with you so that His abiding presence is always with you. I have to tell you, however, that this gift doesn't come cheap. Most of us have to engage in some fervent prayer and do some serious housecleaning before our homes are a fit place for our Lord to dwell. Remember, God is very particular about the company He keeps. He will not live with sin and evil.

Down through the years, and long before the revival ever moved in our church in Pensacola, we have had to discipline some members. We said, "Look, you are free to come to this church if you want to, but you are not going to carry a card saying that you are a member of this church if you continue doing this and that in your life." If people were involved in an adulterous affair, were living a homosexual lifestyle, or were entangled in other evident sins that they would not forsake and repent of, we obeyed the Bible and disciplined them. If they still refused to forsake and repent of their willful sin, then we refused to even eat a meal with them. If a man wanted a position of leadership or authority in the church, we wanted to know how he ruled his household. Scripture says,

For if a man know not how to rule his own house, how shall he take care of the church of God? (1 Timothy 3:5)

My friend, I still believe in holiness because the Bible says that "without holiness no man will see God."[2] God will not move in our churches until we deal with the sin, rebellion, sexual promiscuity, and other unholy habits that permeate our lives. Such behavior hurts our Christian witness and testimony and brings reproach to the name of the Lord. It causes dryness to develop in our worship, prayer, and preaching. Gradually God's Spirit becomes so grieved that He leaves us to enjoy the sin we have preferred over Him, and the spiritual atmosphere in our homes and churches becomes so dry that folks can't stand it.

Joshua confidently crossed the River Jordan armed with a promise from God, but hidden sin cut short God's provision, protection, and blessing! After the Israelites had completely destroyed the great fortified city of Jericho, Joshua sent a smaller group to wipe out a tiny city called Ai. He was shocked when the outnumbered men of that city totally humiliated Joshua's army! When he started complaining to God about "failed promises," the Lord told him to get off of his face. Then the Lord told Joshua that he had better deal with sin in the camp if he expected Jehovah to fight on his behalf. Look what God told Joshua:

> *Therefore the children of Israel could not stand before their enemies, but turned their backs before their enemies, because they were accursed: **neither will I be with you any more**, except ye destroy the accursed from among you. Up, sanctify the people, and say, Sanctify yourselves against tomorrow: for thus saith the Lord God of Israel, There is an accursed thing in the midst of thee, O Israel: thou canst not stand before thine enemies, until ye take away the accursed thing from among you* (Joshua 7:12-13).

God was unmerciful to a man who was ignorant. He said, "I won't be with you anymore except you deal with the sin. Get up and get to it!"

6. *Atonement for the House*

Spiritual problems require spiritual solutions. God was serious about the power and the reality in the spirit realm that these demon gods pointed to. Demon gods are lightning rods for demonic activity. It was this activity that warned of the demonic presence, that prompted God to warn His people so strongly of the need to examine their houses and cleanse them as necessary.

> *And he shall take **to cleanse the house** two birds, and cedar wood, and scarlet, and hyssop: and he shall kill the one of the birds... and he shall take the cedar wood, and the hyssop, and the scarlet, and the living bird, and **dip them in the blood** of the slain bird, and in the running water, and sprinkle the house seven times: and he shall **cleanse the house with the blood** of the bird, and with the running water, and with the living bird, and with the cedar wood, and with the hyssop, and with the scarlet: but he shall **let go the living bird out of the city** into the open fields, and **make an atonement for the house**: and it shall be clean* (Leviticus 14:49-53).

Where demonic contamination was found, God demanded more than mere human cleanup efforts. He demanded *atonement*, which means "to cover over."[3] (It has also been said that atonement means "at-one-ment" with God.) Atonement was always made through the blood of an innocent sacrifice to highlight the horror of man's sin. After the sacrifice of atonement for a contaminated house had been made, the priest was to take hyssop (a bitter herb), dip it in the blood of the slain sacrifice, and sprinkle it over the bare soil where the contaminated house had once stood. This ceremony of atonement had to be performed to cleanse the site where a contaminated residence had been destroyed. No new house could be built there until atonement had been made.

The Law of Moses required that a sacrifice of atonement be offered for every contaminated house. In other words, if there was sin, there had to be blood, innocent blood. Until that blood was shed, the house could not be cleansed in the spirit realm. Whatever contamination the priest found had to be completely removed and atoned for before a "clean" home could again be established there. Fretting leprosy always meant that something was wrong— both in the physical realm and in the spirit realm. If you have appendicitis, you experience symptoms of fever and pain in your body. If you focus on treating just the fever or the body pain, you could lose your life! The fever and pain are merely symptoms of a deeper and far more serious problem. There are symptoms in your home that are just as real and just as dangerous as the physical symptoms of a serious disease. Something is not right. Don't keep ignoring the symptoms.

The Holy Ghost wants me to warn some of you who are reading this book, "There is fretting leprosy in your house, sir. Dear lady, there is fretting leprosy in your house. You are suffering from a sterile environment in your home just as surely as the Israelites suffered when green and red streaks appeared along the walls of their houses. You may not be able to see the contamination beneath the multiple layers of paint and wallpaper you've placed on the walls, but this does not change that fact that something is there. Something in your house has to go if you want the anointing and presence of God to fill you every day and stay with you no matter where you are."

Is the Priest On Duty?

If you are a husband or father, I want you to read these words very carefully: *God has called you to be the priest in your home.* If something isn't right, don't bury your head in the newspaper and act like everything is fine. When your wife or children come to you with a concern about the family, listen to them and take an active role in addressing their concerns. By bringing their cares to you, they are instinctively following God's ancient pattern. They are taking their problems to the priest. They want and need you to stand up and be a man.

Get up and examine your house! See if the wall of protection around your family has holes in it or has been breached in any way. Rid your home of the devil if he has taken up residence there. Get the snake out of your house. You may need to declare, "There is no rest here. We are backbiting and bickering and fussing all the time. This has to stop. As the priest in this home, I am going to rise up, stand watch, and take my duties seriously. I'm going to look at the walls and foundations of every room with a magnifying glass, if I have to. But I won't be quiet until I find out what is here that shouldn't be here." Friend, you won't have to search for long. The Holy Spirit will give you discernment that will lead you right to the plague that is in your house. He may show you contamination in one or both of two areas: the house or its occupants.

1. *Take inventory of your home.*

Let the Holy Spirit guide you. He will impress on your spirit those things that are grieving and offending Him. He may point out where you are dabbling in questionable activities and illicit things that you would never have tolerated in the past. Or He may warn you of habits and activities that have been part of your home for so many years that you've become inoculated to them. Whatever He shows you, thoroughly cleanse every area. If you don't follow through, confessing every problem area and cleaning your house completely, you will soon find that you have lost God's revival fire. In time you may even backslide—all because you did not deal with the plagues in your house that the Holy Spirit revealed to you. If this happens and other believers see you in the mall or at the grocery store, don't tell them that you stopped coming to church because you just got busy. Tell them the truth. They will know what happened—that you wouldn't clean your house so the Lord's anointing could dwell there. Clean your house well so that uncleanness finds no welcome there.

A perpetually unclean house becomes like a leech from the devil. It draws the anointing right out of your life as the leech gets fatter and fatter, and you get weaker and weaker! This is why Paul said that we should "...lay aside every weight, and the sin which doth so easily beset us."[4] God wants to empower you with the boldness to do all that needs to be done in your home. He will not give you rest until you attack everything that opens you and your family to the devil's influence.

2. *Let the occupants of your house examine themselves and the company they keep.*

Sunday night activities is a good place to start. Do you get together with friends after church is over—or do you go home, break out the cola and potato chips, pull off your shoes, prop up your feet—and start critically analyzing the church service? Some Christians may call this fellowship, but I doubt that the Holy Ghost would use that term. The problem is that not only are you enjoying the snacks in your hand but you are also feasting on "roast preacher" for the main course and "baked worship leader" as a side dish, with liberal portions of fricasseed choir members, elders, and deacons added as the trimmings. Sometimes you may even polish it all off with "pastor's wife flambé" or "over-zealous youth pastor on ice." Obviously you prayed and asked God to bless your meal, but you should know very well that He would never bless such a mess. It's not a meal, it's a lynching party; and we all do it in the name of fellowship.

Sunday is not the only time such messy meals take place in your home. Perhaps you spend every evening meal picking apart your boss or your coworkers. Maybe your favorite stew is seasoned with biting criticism directed at your spouse or your children. On the other hand, sinful words motivated by jealousy, hatred, envy, bitterness, dissension, disrespect, or lust may add spice to your food. God cannot and will not bless your meals (or your home) when your attitudes, conversation, or behavior reveal that sinful company, pleasures, or habits are contaminating you.

Your Words Contain Power

Jesus said,

> *The words that I speak unto you, they are spirit, and they are life* (John 6:63b).

Can the same be said of your words? Too often, I fear, your answer needs to be, "The words I speak are spirit, and they are death!"

Words are powerful forces. They reveal what is in your heart. Jesus said,

> *A good man out of the good treasure of his heart bringeth forth that which is good; and an evil man out of the evil treasure of his heart bringeth forth that which is evil: for of the abundance of the heart his mouth speaketh* (Luke 6:45).

What you say comes from your innermost belly. Thus your words embody the condition of your spirit. As your words leave your mouth, the "spirit" of what you just said fills the air and begins to rumble around in your home. Whether for good or for evil, they take up residence in your home, your workplace, your church—wherever you are when you speak the words. Like bubbles of air, your words burst and begin to affect the atmosphere. Caustic, biting, negative words spew destructive influences into your environment. Loving, affirming, considerate words, on the other hand, enrich your environment and keep it fluid and free.

These influences or spirits then move from one person to the next, to the next, to the next, and so on. The Bible speaks of this "transference of spirits":

> *And the Lord came down in a cloud, and spake unto [Moses], and **took of the spirit that was upon him, and gave it unto the seventy elders:** and it came to pass, that, when the spirit rested upon them, they prophesied, and did not cease* (Numbers 11:25).

The same influence in the negative occurred totally apart from God's blessing when the spirit of doubt, fear, and unbelief saturated the ten fearful spies who returned from the Promised Land. These negative spirits were transferred to the entire nation of Israel![5] The result of this negative transference was that all but two of the adult members of that nation were barred from entering the land God had promised to give them. They died as desert wanderers because they had accepted the negative spirit of the ten spies who misled them.

The words you speak in your home are "spirit." The same is true for all the words that others speak there. They release whatever is in them as surely as the sun rises each morning. What they set free is up to you. Your words and the words of others who enter your home loose either blessings or curses upon your household. You may be used to having lots of alternative choices, but God clearly provides only two:

I call heaven and earth to record this day against you, that I have set before you life and death, blessing and cursing: therefore choose life, that both thou and thy seed may live (Deuteronomy 30:19).

There are no alternatives. The words we choose to speak release either life or death into our homes. That's it. Period. If we are wise, we will carefully guard the words that come both from our mouths and the mouths of all persons who live in our homes. Exercising authority over every word that comes into our homes, we will also monitor the words that we permit others to speak when they are visiting us. If you find yourself telling your spouse when your friends pull out of the driveway, "I don't know why, but every time they come for a visit, I feel like I need a bath when they leave," you would do well to consider carefully the words, the spirits, that they are introducing into your home. Most likely they are condemning your pastor, criticizing your church, ridiculing God's revival fire, or describing the move of His Spirit as a work of the flesh.

If your friends are always critical or doubtful about the things of God, if they are constantly slandering and gossiping about God's people, here is my pastoral counsel for you: Don't invite them back into your home. "Oh, but we have been friends for years," you may say. Perhaps it is time to reconsider that friendship. Every minute you spend in their company gives them the opportunity to transfer their negative attitudes, thoughts, and be-havior onto you.

Difficult as it may be, you must be careful never to put rela-tionships above principle, or people above God's Word. To do so is the same thing as calling the local trash dump and arranging for them to fill your living room with a load of fresh garbage. The scents from whatever smelly rubbish was thrown into the garbage will soon permeate your entire house. The same is true of your children's friends. Watch who you let your youth hang out with and bring into your home.

You can choose to live with the stench if you want to, but I must warn you that you should also be prepared for the sterility that will overtake your house. Rotting garbage has a way of leaving a lingering odor. Evil words and ungodly companions have a simi-lar effect. When you allow them into your home, you soon find that the environment in which you live destroys life instead of re-newing it.

You must make the choice. Will you choose an atmosphere that refreshes, preserves, encourages, and renews you and all who enter your home, or will you occupy a sterile, lifeless house that is dominated by anger, strife, sorrow, and death? You cannot blame others for whatever you choose, since you alone have the authority to censor what happens in your home.

God has given you every tool you need to establish a home filled with laughter, peace, respect, and love. He has made you a priest and a king through Jesus Christ.[6] Now you must put all He has given you to good use. You must obey His Word and yield to the leading of His Spirit. When you are truly tired of living under brassy skies in a sterile house, no effort, no sacrifice, will be too great to rid yourself of the leprosy that has invaded your home. Only then will you be ready to stand in Jesus' name and do some-thing about the plague that has overcome you.

It's time to clean house! God is waiting at the door. As you sweep all the negative talk, idolatrous loyalties, and ungodly habits out the door, He will enter and fill every room of your home with the sweetness of His Spirit and the power of His anointing. This, I guarantee, is what your heart has been longing for.

Remember, God will not leave His revival Spirit in the Church very long if we don't go home and clean house. It would be a double standard. He will lift His Spirit and write *Ichabod*—the glory has departed—over the door. I don't know about you, but I'm going to do everything in my power to protect the Dove so that it won't be grieved or offended in my home or the church I pastor. I don't want the Dove to fly.

Endnotes

1. See Deuteronomy 6:10-11.
2. See Hebrews 12:14.
3. *Strong's*, **kaphar** (Heb., #3722).
4. Hebrews 12:1a.
5. See Numbers 13:26–14:4.
6. See Revelation 1:6.

Chapter 7

Opening the Heavens Over Your Home

You deserve what you tolerate.

I heard something a long time ago that I am going to pass on to you: *You deserve what you tolerate!* I have never forgotten this, and I hope that you never forget it either. If you get a mole right at your belt line so that every time you walk, your clothing rubs against it and it irritates you, don't complain to your spouse saying, "Oh honey, this thing is so sore and irritated. Will you draw me a bath?" Go to the doctor and have it removed! If you choose not to do this, you deserve every bit of irritation it gives you!

This truth is applicable to many areas of life. If you let your kids sass you and defy you to your face, don't complain, "I just can't do anything with this child." You are getting what you deserve. Indeed, things will continue to get worse until you take action to change the child's behavior. Firm discipline with love, be that taking a paddle and administering corporal punishment or applying some other form of effective correction, is the only solution to your problem. (I know that will require you to trust God's Word more than the failed child-rearing theories of man, but your child will not change until you firmly put your foot down.)

One time a man came into my office. He was a big fellow, but when he sat down, he just started crying like a baby. "Brother Kilpatrick," he said, "can you help us? My boy out there, I can't do anything with him." First I looked at this man and his wife (they were very distinguished-looking people); then I looked out into the foyer at an old sourpuss of a teenager who was sitting there. The boy was quite a bit smaller than his father, so I said, "You're telling me you can't do anything with your boy. Before I say anything else, let me ask you a question: Did you ever spank him when you were raising him?"

That huge man looked down at his big hands and said, "Well, no. Why? Now you gotta understand..." I had heard all that I needed to hear. I just told the man to take his son home. Friend, *don't bring your neglected child to the preacher and expect him to correct the omissions of the father!* The buck stops with you. You are responsible for his behavior.

The brassy heavens over your head and the fretting plague in your house will never be removed *until you are ready to stop tolerating the reality and the consequences of the sin in your life.* When you are ready to end the devil's rampage in your life and your home by obeying God, He will undertake for you and blast satan from his position of influence. There are six steps you must take to purge your house and clear the heavens. I like to summarize them as questions:
1. Is there disorder in your home?
2. Are you robbing God?
3. Are you speaking blessings or curses in your house?
4. Is there anything in your home that holds power over you?
5. Is your home under a curse?
6. Is satan saddling up the airwaves and riding into your home through the television?

Once you decide that you will no longer tolerate brassy heavens over your head or plagues in your house, it is time to assess the condition of your home. The careful consideration of each question listed above can help you do that. Depending on the answers to those questions, you may need to take the six corresponding steps to reestablishing freedom and holiness.

Jesus described satan's intentions when He said,

The thief cometh not, but for to steal, and to kill, and to destroy (John 10:10a).

These goals all require that satan first gain access to your house. Notice that Jesus called satan "a thief."

...He that entereth not by the door into the sheepfold, but climbeth up some other way, the same is a thief and robber. But he that entereth in by the door is the shepherd of the sheep (John 10:1-2).

A thief does not enter your home through the front door like an invited guest does. He looks for some other way to get into your house. Don't expect satan to use a different tactic when he visits you. He is now a thief, has always been a thief, and will remain a thief. Right now he is looking for an open window, an unguarded passageway, or a breech in the wall through which he can force his way into your home.

Some homes have many access routes for satan to use. Each of the questions you just used to evaluate the condition of your own home suggests ways in which satan can gain access to violate your family. If you answered yes to any of these questions, you are giving the devil ready access to your home. Let's look at each question in turn to help you assess how freely the devil is coming against you to do his death-producing work. We will pay particular attention to the first question, since this is often satan's mode of entrance when the more obvious alternatives are not available.

1. Is there disorder in your home? Reestablish God's order.

God has set a divine order for the home (and the Church). When this order is in place and functioning well, satan often begins his sinister attack by trying to create disorder so that he can catch you unawares. This is particularly true when the home is well guarded and the man of the house is doing a good job as the priest. Satan will not assault the man's authority directly, but will attempt to subvert his authority by attacking another member of the household.

This mode of operation is clearly demonstrated in the Book of Genesis. Satan did not go to Adam and attempt to lead him astray; he first went to Eve. Like the thief he is, the evil one circumvented the head of the first family. Once satan had convinced Eve to disobey God, it was much easier to get Adam to sin too. He didn't even approach Adam directly, but sent Eve instead. The resulting sequence of events shows that disorder is usually followed by doubt, denial, deception, disobedience, division, and death.

Disorder Comes First

The Bible clearly states that the man is to be the head of the home.

Head of the Man
But I would have you know, that the head of every man is Christ; and the head of the woman is the man; and the head of Christ is God (1 Corinthians 11:3).

Contrary to many erroneous teachings, the husband's position as the head of the home does not make him superior to the woman. Just as God the Father, Jesus Christ the Son, and the Holy Spirit are all one but with distinct functions and characteristics, so husbands and wives are one with differing functions and characteristics. Likewise, just as it is inconceivable that we would try to separate the Trinity, so we should not try to separate the husband/wife team. A man and his wife are to be one in every way. They simply have differing roles and responsibilities in the home. A woman is not inferior to her husband. Her role and position are not of lesser value or importance. They are merely different. Truly her place under the authority of her husband is God's plan for protecting her and their home.

Head of the Woman
Submitting yourselves one to another in the fear of God. Wives, submit yourselves unto your own husbands, as unto the Lord. **For the husband is the head of the wife, even as Christ is the head of the**

church: *and He is the saviour of the body. Therefore as the church is subject unto Christ, so let the wives be to their own husbands in every thing. Husbands, love your wives, even as Christ also loved the church, and gave Himself for it* (Ephesians 5:21-25).

Jesus carefully maintained a right relationship with His head. He did nothing that He did not first see His Father doing.[1] This was a priority for Jesus because the power and authority to fulfill His mission were directly linked to His unity of purpose, mind, and spirit with God the Father.

A man and a woman united in a marriage relationship need the same unity of purpose, mind, and spirit. When this unity is missing, both husband and wife are open to the guiles of satan. In a similar manner, satan gains access to our homes when both husband and wife assume either the man's or the woman's roles. God created the man to conquer and rule and placed him as the head of the home to protect it. The woman, on the other hand, was carefully designed by God to bear children and to nurture the family in tenderness. When either the protective, conquering role or the tender, nurturing role is missing in a home because the husband and wife have confused or abdicated their particular roles, disorder results, since each role is precious and vital for the family's well-being. Unfortunately, the tempter knows how prone we are in today's society to rank one role higher than the other, so he uses this weakness for his gain and our loss.

Had Adam and Eve been clear and strong in their roles, Eve would have deferred to her husband, the protector, when the serpent came around. As the protector, Adam was equipped with the authority and power to deal with enemy. Instead of permitting the serpent to deceive Eve, Adam should have done something to prevent the ensuing tragedy. He should have moved in his authority and rebuked that snake. Instead, like many husbands today, Adam did nothing and sin entered our world. Because of this disorder—Eve was first deceived, then Adam knowingly sinned—satan gained authority that rightly belonged to Adam and Eve. He used this authority to take his deceptive plan a step further. Disorder gave way to doubt.

After Disorder Comes Doubt

Once satan had successfully bypassed Adam, creating disorder in the family, he began to plant doubt in Eve's mind. Carefully he unfolded his deceptive plan, using the words, "hath God said...?" These words clouded Eve's memory as she tried to recall exactly what God had said.

> *Now the serpent was more subtle than any beast of the field which the Lord God had made. And he said unto the woman, Yea, **hath God said**, Ye shall not eat of every tree of the garden?* (Genesis 3:1)

The adversary tries the same tactic with us. Think for a moment what happens when someone questions the accuracy of how you remember someone else's words. If you are like most people, you wrinkle your brow for a minute and critically scan your memory to make sure that what you said matches what you heard. Just the asking of the question plants doubt that you did not hear correctly or recount correctly the original speaker's words. This doubt must be overcome.

Satan knew full well what God had said. So did the woman until satan asked the question, "Hath God said...?" Only then did doubt enter. When God spoke to the man and the woman, they believed what they heard, having no reason to doubt. God had spoken. That was it. Period. With satan's question, what had once been a closed discussion suddenly became open to interpretation. By suggesting that there was a possible alternative to what Eve thought God had said, satan put a question mark in Eve's mind about God's word.

This is always satan's way. God speaks with authority, putting a period after His word because it is fixed, final, and unchangeable. Satan, on the other hand, operates in the realm of question marks. He wants us to regard God's commands differently so that we are not so likely to obey them implicitly. In truth, He wants us to think that God's Word shifts and changes depending on circumstance.

Then we are more likely to give in to our passing whims and desires until we no longer obey what God has commanded or believe what He has promised. For example, the Scriptures clearly state that satan's eternal damnation and punishment are inevitable because of the victory Christ won on the cross. The enemy, however, is so skillful at deception that he has convinced many that there is no eternal damnation and punishment—for him or for them. My friend, don't be deceived. Doubt is always a prelude to denial.

After Doubt Comes Denial

> *And the woman said unto the serpent, We may eat of the fruit of the trees of the garden: but of the fruit of the tree which is in the midst of the garden,* **God hath said,** *Ye shall not eat of it, neither shall ye touch it, lest ye die. And* **the serpent said** *unto the woman,* **Ye shall not surely die** (Genesis 3:2-4).*

After satan stuck a knife into Eve's faith in God, causing her to doubt His words, he gave the knife a twist by openly contradicting God's words: "Ye shall not surely die." By denying God's words, he implied that he had inside knowledge about God's motives. In other words, he was saying, "God didn't really say that you would die."

Make no mistake about it. If satan can keep you doubting long enough, he will eventually lead you into denial. This puts you in a very vulnerable position, since once he has placed doubt in your mind about one thing, he works around the clock to attack other areas of your life: your marriage, your children, your friends, your church family, your coworkers, your boss. Each of these relationships becomes a target area where the great deceiver attempts to plant doubt so that he can lead you into denial. Should his plan succeed, you will eventually deny everything you hold dear, including your loved ones, your faith in God, and even your salvation through the Lord Jesus Christ.

Beware lest you tolerate the doubt satan plants in your mind, for doubt leads to denial, which then leads to deception. Satan has no inside information; he just wants you to believe that he does!

After Denial Comes Deception

Deception is the process of rejecting truth in favor of a lie. Satan's ultimate lie is that God's motives are different from what He knows and says they are.

> *And the serpent said unto the woman, Ye shall not surely die.* **For God doth know** *that in the day ye eat thereof, then your eyes shall be opened, and* **ye shall be as gods, knowing good and evil.** *And when the woman saw that the tree was good for food, and that it was pleasant to the eyes, and* **a tree to be desired** *to make one wise...* (Genesis 3:4-6).

Once the serpent had challenged Eve's memory of God's words, causing her to doubt that she had heard correctly, he quickly presumed to speak for God. First He denied that God had meant what He said. Then He inserted words into God's mouth that directly contradicted not only His words but also His intentions. With the words "for God doth know," satan planted in Eve's mind the idea that God was keeping something from her. How subtly the deceiver worked, taking something that was already Eve's and convincing her that it was a forbidden tidbit to be desired, and taking that which was forbidden and making it appear that it was her right to have it.

Satan's plan worked. Within a few short sentences, Eve took the bait. She began to look at the tree of the knowledge of good and evil in a new way. Under the influence of the deceiver, she decided that the tree was "good for food...pleasant to the eyes, and a tree to be desired to make one wise." In fact, it was none of the above.

Eve's deception led to Adam's deception. He also took satan's bait, although he knew better. Once satan gets you to believe that wrong is right and right is wrong, he is well on the way to damning you—and not only you, but those you live with, play with, work with, and worship with. Our culture is rapidly converting to this upside-down view of life. It is no wonder that America is full of deceived, disobedient people.

After Deception Comes Disobedience

> *And when the woman saw...* **she took** *of the fruit thereof, and did eat,* **and gave also unto her husband** *with her; and he did eat* (Genesis 3:6).

Deception invariably leads to disobedience, which is refusing to obey and partaking of forbidden things. People who are living in disobedience believe that they can make it work out in the end. They think that they can "have their cake and eat it too." Sin and death now become experiential knowledge (Hebrew *yada*) because they believe that they can sin like the devil in this life and talk their way into Saint Peter's gate when the time comes. So thoroughly does satan pervert their understanding of right and wrong that they develop a distorted perception of God Himself. "If God is a good God," they say, "He would never send me to hell." The problem with this is that God is not like man. He does not lie. He says what He means, and means what He says. Once He says something, there is no room for discussion, negotiation, or special privileges.

King Saul learned this the hard way. He thought that God would bend the rule of righteousness just for him. He soon found out that transgression equals disobedience, no matter how you look at it or try to justify it.

> ...*Behold,* **to obey is better than sacrifice,** *and to hearken than the fat of rams. For* **rebellion is as the sin of witchcraft,** *and stubbornness is as iniquity and idolatry. Because thou hast* **rejected the word** *of the Lord,* **He hath also rejected thee**... (1 Samuel 15:22-23).

After Disobedience Comes Division

More than half of American marriages end in divorce because division has crept into the home. Adam and Eve experienced this division that follows disobedience. When God asked Adam to explain what had happened, Adam started pointing fingers of blame and division. In a few words, "that woman You gave me," Adam accused both God and Eve of being the reason for Adam's disobedience.

Adam pointed the accusing finger everywhere but where it belonged—toward himself. In that moment his oneness with the helpmate God had given him, and with his Creator, were lost. Sin had separated Adam and Eve from each other, from God, and as they would soon learn, from their paradise home. This consequence of sin applied not only to Adam and Eve, but to every man and woman since them. Their appetite for one bite of forbidden fruit earned the entire human race a sentence of death, as God drove them from the garden so that they wouldn't eat of the tree of life and be stuck forever in their fallen state.

We are no different from Adam and Eve. Our willful disobedience affects not only us, but every member of our family. Indeed this point of division is often where our children are also caught in satan's deceptive scheme.

Head of the Children

Children, obey your parents in the Lord: for this is right. Honour thy father and mother; which is the first commandment with promise; that it may be well with thee, and **thou mayest live long on the earth.** *And, ye fathers, provoke not your children to wrath: but bring them up in the nurture and admonition of the Lord* (Ephesians 6:1-4).

When Mom and Dad are separated—either physically separated so that they live in separate households, or emotionally separated so that they live in the same house but do what they want, when they want, with no concern for the other marriage partner's needs and wishes—children become caught up in satan's death-producing tactics. At first they may avoid obedience by pitting one parent against another: "Mom said..." or "Dad lets me...." Over time this degenerates to the point where the child takes one parent's side or emotionally withdraws from the other parent.

Even in relatively healthy households where the parents are not separated, they must be careful to present a united front to their children. Should they neglect to do this, the child may be deceived into believing that obedience is optional. Now the entire family is deprived of the love, peace, and joy that God originally planned for the well-being of every human family. The death of the family unit as God designed it is inevitable when sin and disobedience lead to separation and division. Trust is broken, loyalties are divided, and loving fellowship and support are lost as all members of the family succumb to the delusion of individual autonomy. Obedience becomes a thing of the past.

After Division Comes Death

> But now being made free from sin, and become servants to God, ye have your fruit unto holiness, and the end everlasting life. **For the wages of sin is death; but the gift of God is eternal life through Jesus Christ our Lord** (Romans 6:22-23).

Death reigns where there is disorder, doubt, denial, deception, disobedience, and division. Don't forget that it all starts with disorder. When we are not in the proper alignment with God and our fellowman, death is inevitable. Either we see no reason to stay within God's divine order, or else the downward spiral toward death has been going on for so long that we do not even realize that we are out of order.

Restoring God's order in our homes requires that we work our way back, undoing each step that led to our family's demise. Obedience is thus often the first thing we must restore. Any home where rebellion is tolerated will show evidence of defilement and decay. You can believe the foolish theories of rebellious college professors and fanciful pediatricians if you want to, but having order in your house is important to God. That popular magazine or TV talk show "expert" may say that your disobedient children are just going through a phase, but my Bible says that one of the signs of the coming of the Lord in the last days is that children shall rise up against their parents in disobedience and destruction.[2] Sometimes we pay attention to everybody but God, and we are paying a hellish price for it.

One look at our public schools and the state of our homes tells the story. Disobedience among our youth is a sign of the times. This disobedience, however, does not have to be found in your home. Your kids may try to be disobedient to you, but the only way they will succeed is if you tolerate it.

I grew up without a father in the house. My mother was just under five feet tall, but when she went outside for a switch to correct the error of my ways, I knew that I was about to suffer the consequences of my disobedience. In truth, I had a godly fear of my mother, although for many of my growing-up years I was more than two feet taller than she was!

Before I ever thought about being bad, I always thought about Mama. She used to make me drag my six-foot frame outside to our peach tree to cut off a switch for my correction. When I'd come back with some anemic, puny excuse for a switch that wouldn't even cut the air, she would send me back out again, saying, "No boy, you get back out there and cut a decent switch." When I came back with a second switch, I would say, "Mama, I got you a good one!" hoping that I would touch her heart with my newly found zeal. It never quite worked that way, for Mama would always say, "Bend over, boy." That was when I knew that my sin had found me out and my fate was sealed.

When Mama was done with me, I had no trouble rightly discerning right from wrong. If my memory got bad, my bottom reminded me of the straight and narrow. I respected my mother with a healthy fear, but I also loved her dearly. That mixture of fear and love has had a profound impact on my relationship with God. I have a healthy fear of God today because I developed a healthy fear of my mother in my early years. I tell young people, "If you do not have a healthy respect for your dad and mom, you will never respect your schoolteacher or your principal. Neither will you respect a policeman, a judge, the authority of your church, or God Himself with a healthy fear. A lack of fearing God is a sure ticket to hell."

Sometimes parents tell me that they love their children and don't want to lose their friendship by spanking or correcting them. I tell them, "Listen, God did not call you to be a friend to those kids. He called you to be a parent." Parents have to tell their kids the truth, not just what they want to hear. It never crossed my mind to wonder whether my kids liked me or not. All I knew was that I wanted peace in my home. That will never happen if you don't administer a spanking once in a while in *moderation and love*.

My boys will testify today that I occasionally had to spank them. Before I spanked one of my sons, I always read the Bible to him, being careful to show him in the Scriptures why I had to administer corporal punishment. Then I would spank him exactly like I had promised. A few minutes after I had spanked him, I would take my boy into my lap and love him. While I loved him and hugged him close, I'd say, "Son, I love you so much. That is why I had to correct you." Then I would drive off in my car and cry. Every single time I went to a certain secluded spot to cry. That was my pattern: I read the Word, spanked my boy, loved him, then cried in my time alone.

Today my boys are strong committed Christians. They love God and they respect my authority, even as grown men. Before my oldest son had married and moved out of the house, I told him one time, "Son, I'd appreciate it if you wouldn't work on Sunday. I don't approve of you working on Sundays because God has commanded that you should not work on the Sabbath[3] and 'the ox is not in the ditch,'[4] which is the only time God allowed His people to work on the Sabbath. If you honor the Lord in this way, He will one day bless you with a good job. Make the right decision now, Scott."

He said, "Okay, Dad." Sure enough, God opened up a great job for him. He is doing well supporting his family, and they have a new home. Indeed, God has really blessed him because he honored his father and the Word of the Lord.

Disobedience in your home causes the heavens over your head to become brass. It separates you from God and His blessings. A pattern of disobedience also separates you from the members of your family. Trust, love, and mutual encouragement and support are lost. It pays to demand obedience in your home.

2. Are you robbing God? Rid your house of dishonesty and of falsely gained wealth.

Will a man rob God? Yet ye have robbed Me. But ye say, Wherein have we robbed Thee? In tithes and offerings. Ye are cursed with a curse: for ye have robbed Me, even this whole nation (Malachi 3:8-9).

Through the prophet Malachi, God promised that He would open the windows of Heaven over those who give Him tithes and offerings. He also warned that the heavens would be closed over those who chose to rob Him by withholding these. Now I have to tell you that this principle goes far beyond tithes and offerings. God's warning against robbing Him covers every imaginable type of greed and lust for money because greed and holiness do not mix!

You do well then, as you assess the condition of your home and take the corrective steps to restore holiness and freedom, to consider if you are withholding from God or others what rightly belongs to them.

Is there *dishonest* gain in your home? Are you hiding and hoarding gambling money, stolen property, lottery tickets, or money laundered from unholy sources? That money has spiritual toxins on it! It was gained the wrong way. Look at these powerful Scriptures:

Wealth gotten by vanity shall be diminished: but he that gathereth by labour shall increase (Proverbs 13:11).

An inheritance may be gotten hastily at the beginning; but the end thereof shall not be blessed (Proverbs 20:21).

Is there *hidden* gain in your house? Are you tucking away untaxed money that you've hidden from the government to avoid paying your fair share of taxes? Are you clinging to an unshared inheritance or keeping a larger portion than your kin have received? Such gain brings a curse upon your house. I've seen otherwise godly people just "go to the devil" when a family inheritance goes to probate court. They have come under the power of the devil and are bowing their knees to the false god of mammon—much to the detriment of their Christian witness! I've personally known many good families who were destroyed by greed over what Mama and Daddy left in their wills.

Perhaps you deliberately deceive your parents, your spouse, or your children so that you can amass wealth at their expense. God knows what you are doing. He will repay you for your iniquity. Perhaps your dishonesty extends to God's tithe. You are selfishly keeping what belongs to the Lord. Beware! I firmly believe that with the coming of revival fire we will also see the restoration of the immediate, visible judgment of God such as was seen in Acts 5, when Ananias and Sapphira were struck dead for lying to the Holy Spirit! Dishonesty does not pay! Clean your house of all lying, deception, and dishonesty, no matter what the cause or form. This is a second step for restoring open heavens over your home.

3.   Are you speaking blessings or curses in your house? Speak words of blessing.

Jesus said,

The words that I speak unto you, they are spirit, and they are life (John 6:63b).

As we saw in the previous chapter, our words carry power. That power can bring either life or death. This puts much responsibility squarely on our shoulders to consider carefully the impact of our words. This is particularly true for the man of the house, as he safeguards or reestablishes the holiness of his home. If you are a man, you are responsible for the atmosphere created by the words that you permit to be spoken in your home.

Psalm 19:14 says,

Let the words of my mouth, and the meditation of my heart, be acceptable in Thy sight, O Lord, my strength, and my redeemer.

We need to remember that our mouths are continually releasing either blessings or curses into our environments. Curses are things that we don't want to come to pass, yet we speak them anyway. I used to equate the biblical concepts of prophecy and blessing. Now I know that there is a big difference between prophecy and blessing. Both are of God, but few have the power to prophecy. Everyone has the power to bless.

Even our prayers fall under this principle of blessing and cursing. At one point in my ministry, God admonished me that I was actually praying curses over my church. Because I was constantly complaining and whining that my vision for the church wasn't coming to pass, my words were accomplishing the opposite of what I yearned for. In a similar manner, I often listed my lacks during my prayer time, instead of thanking God for His goodness, power, and mercy to accomplish what I could not.

One day the Holy Spirit showed me my error. From that time on, I began to pray the solution instead of the problem. I began to speak into existence those things that were not. Sure enough, I began to see those things come to pass in God's timing. It took some time for me to learn to pray blessings instead of curses. During that time, the Holy Spirit, my Teacher, taught me much from God's Word.

Family Blessings

The more I studied and read, the more I realized that everyone in the Old Testament was in the blessing business. In fact, a father's blessing was so important that it was considered the most valuable part of a son's inheritance. This was particularly true for the eldest son, who inherited most of his father's property. Having already given his younger brother, Jacob, his birthright, Esau was quite distraught when he discovered that Jacob had also received their father's blessing. "...Hast thou but one blessing, my father? bless me, even me also, O my father..."[5] were his pitiful words as he wept inconsolably.

When Jacob neared the end of his life, He blessed his sons with fatherly blessings that followed them the rest of their lives. Speaking to each one individually, he spoke powerful things that called into being things that were not yet visible.

A similar blessing is evident in the love story of Isaac and Rebekah as told in Genesis 24. As Rebekah is about to leave with Abraham's servant to become Isaac's wife, Laban and Bethuel gather the entire family around Rebekah and declare with all the power of the biblical blessing as God ordained it,

...Thou art our sister, be thou the mother of thousands of millions, and let thy seed possess the gate of those which hate them (Genesis 24:60).

How different might our daughters' lives be if we blessed them in this way as they entered a marriage covenant. How many presidents, prime ministers, generals, and other world leaders would be born into our families in the years to come?

Priestly Blessings

The New Testament also makes it clear that God wants His people to practice a lifestyle of blessing.

Bless them which persecute you; bless, and curse not (Romans 12:14).
This is particularly evident in that Jesus, when He sent out His disciples, commanded them to bless those homes where they were received warmly and treated graciously.

*And into whatsoever house ye enter, first say, **Peace be to this house.** And if the son of peace be there, **your peace shall rest upon it**: if not, it shall turn to you again* (Luke 10:5-6).

He then went on to say that if a city received them well, miracles and gifts of healing would manifest in that place. But if the inhabitants rejected the Lord's servants, they were authorized to pronounce a curse on that city!

This type of a priestly blessing is one of the most wonderful gifts a man or woman of God can give God's people from the pulpit. Powerful examples of priestly blessings begin nearly every Epistle in the New Testament. This blessing is given as God comes upon us with unction (or anointing) to speak the things that we desire for the people over which we are speaking. In truth, this is what a blessing is. It possesses the creative power of God Himself.

Speaking Blessings or Curses in Our Homes

One thing the Bible is also clear about is that blessing and cursing should never come from the same mouth. The words we utter, whether in blessing or in cursing, are what will return to us.

Out of the same mouth proceedeth blessing and cursing. My brethren, these things ought not so to be. Doth a fountain send forth at the same place sweet water and bitter? Can the fig tree, my brethren, bear olive berries? either a vine, figs? so can no fountain both yield salt water and fresh (James 3:10-12).

Not rendering evil for evil, or railing for railing: but contrariwise blessing; knowing that ye are thereunto called, that ye should inherit a blessing (1 Peter. 3:9).

Many times we do not realize what good or damage we do with our words. If we want to be blessed, we have to bless. Let me show you what I mean, using the relationship between a parent and a child.

A Father's Curse: "Come here, boy. You make me sick. You're such a deadbeat that you're never going to amount to anything. I guess you're going to get your little girlfriend pregnant. Then I'll have to haul both of you through the rest of your lives. I can already tell that I'm going to have to pay your bills and support your illegitimate child. You're sickening. You're not working, and you never go out and look for a job. Why, you are just the laziest person I've ever known. Other kids get up and do something with their lives. Their parents are real proud of them. But you...you just make me ashamed."

A Mother's Curse: "Come here, girl. Where were you last night? Don't lie to me because I know that you were out there in that guy's car making love. I know that you already lost your virginity. Well, if you think that you're going to have an illegitimate child and bring him into this house, you've got a surprise coming. Don't even bother to go to church with us when that happens. I will not give those women the satisfaction of pointing at you and telling me, 'I told you so'...even if I have always said that you'd end up being a tramp."

Parents who continually speak curses over their children's lives have only themselves to blame when their predictions become self-fulfilling prophecies. What kind of a man will a 16-year-old boy become if his father always curses him, running him down because the father believes that the boy is lazy? What kind of a woman will a teenage daughter become if her mother continually tells her that she is a tramp? How different their lives would be if their parents blessed them, not cursed them. How special would be those times when parents put their hands on their children, thanking the Lord for them and blessing them in His name.

A Father's Blessing: "Come here, son. I want you to know that I love you. I can sense that you are going through a tough time right now. I had to find myself when I was your age, and it wasn't easy. I still remember those rough days I went through. I just want you to know that your mother and I still remember that special day when we took you to the man of God and put you in his arms. Son, that was the day we dedicated you to the Lord. I still remember the prayer that minister prayed over you. I can tell you that I have full faith in God's ability and willingness to bring that prayer to pass! He is the author and finisher of our faith. I guess you know that I can hardly wait one more day for you to have a little family so I can bounce your kids on my knees. Those are going to be great days! But in the meantime, son, as you go through these tough days, remember that your mother and I are standing behind you with everything we've got. Don't hurry into manhood. Let God take you there in His own time. If you ever need to talk to me, you just come to me. After all, you are my son, and I want only the best for you. I'd like to take time right now to ask our Lord to continue blessing you."

A Mother's Blessing: "Come here, my daughter, and let me talk with you. You may not believe it, but I remember how I felt when I was young. I was in a hurry to grow up and marry some handsome young man, and I just couldn't wait to have a baby of my own. Do you know what I discovered? I found out that young girls are supposed to dream of those things. That is the way God made us. After I fell in love with your father and we got married, we both dreamed of a child. What a blessing your birth was for us! Then I realized that God wanted me to be happy even more than I did, and so did my parents. Honey, it's okay to dream about romance and your future husband. Still, it would be even better if you would start praying about them right now. Don't wait until you think you've found your young man. Pray for him now, even before you meet him. At the right time, God will bring you two together. Why don't we pray for that together right now? ... I love you, honey. By the way, you're going to make a great mom."

God longs to see godly fathers and mothers bless their children and each other. Begin today to weigh your words carefully before you release the power they carry. This is one thing you can do immediately to clean up a sterile house. If you've been speaking curses—either purposefully or unintentionally—begin this moment to speak blessings! Ask God to forgive you as you break all the curses you've spoken. Repent and begin a life of blessings.

4. Is there anything in your home that holds power over you? Free your home of the power of sin.

There is a difference between the *penalty of sin* and the *power of sin*. Most Christians worry about the penalty of sin, but they really need to worry more about the power of sin. By concerning themselves primarily with the penalty of sin, they focus more on the outcome of their lives than on the influences in their lives. They work hard to avoid hell, but give little thought to the attitudes, thoughts, and behaviors that sin implants in their lives.

If this is true for you, you may try many things so that you don't get caught cheating—be that on your income tax, your boss, or your spouse—but you do little to change the cheating patterns that have taken over your life. Obviously you have forgotten that you cannot hide your cheating from God. He has caught you whether or not the government, your boss, or your spouse catches you. The trouble with this viewpoint is that your real problem shows up only when you ask yourself, "Why am I hiding this, anyway? What power is causing me to hide what I am doing, to sneak around certain people, to disguise my actions, to lie about my whereabouts...to cheat?" The answer, my friend, is the power of sin. Sin is holding you under its power.

Yes, the penalty of your sin has been dealt with if you have received Jesus Christ as your Savior. His blood covers all that you confess and repent of. Now ask yourself the more basic question and give an honest answer: "Does that particular sin I confessed still exert power over my life?" In other words, are you still lying? Do you still feel driven to expand the truth to justify your behavior? Are you still bitter over a wrong you suffered long ago?

"Well, Brother Kilpatrick," you may say, "I asked God to forgive me because I want to go to Heaven. My sin is now under the blood." This may be true, but you still haven't answered the more important question: Does the sin still have power over you?

Most alcoholics hate what they do. Many of them are quick to repent of the sins they commit when they are drunk. They sincerely ask God to forgive them and to save their souls. This is all very good, but forgiveness does not break the power of the alcoholism. Until this power is broken, they will regularly need to deal with the penalty of their sin. Indeed, if they persist in their alcoholic patterns, they may well end up being worse off than before they asked God to forgive them.

I want you to understand this: God has the power not only to forgive any sins you have committed but also to break every damnable thing that has a death grip on your life. Nothing is too hard for Him! If you are an alcoholic, a drug addict, a child abuser, a pornography addict, a liar, a habitual gambler—a slave to whatever sin has taken over your life—God's Spirit can forever break the chains of that sin so that it no longer exerts power over you. No matter what has you in its grip, be that an eating disorder, a multiple personality disorder, anger, or lust, God can free you for life! Sin shall not have dominion over you.

Let not sin therefore reign in your mortal body, that ye should obey it in the lusts thereof. ... For sin shall not have dominion over you: for ye are not under the law, but under grace (Romans 6:12,14).

Perhaps you are in bondage to the devil himself. I guarantee that you still have the power of choice. You can choose today to confess all your weaknesses, fears, and inabilities to Jesus Christ. You can forsake the sin that has become an unbearable weight. Jesus will meet you as you kneel before Him in surrender. He will unleash the power of Heaven to set you free!

You are a product of your choices. Make the right choices and you will be free, no matter how satan has bound you today and what he tries tomorrow. You can rid your heart and your home of the power of sin. Be careful then to guard all that Jesus has cleansed. This a crucial step in clearing the heavens over your home.

5.   Is your home under a curse? Destroy those things that act as beacons to draw demons to your home.

According to international law, the land, buildings, and property of any foreign embassy, be that in the United States or abroad, is part of that nation. This is why oppressed people under authoritarian regimes, or caught between warring factions, often flee to U.S. embassies and ask for asylum. As long as they stay at the embassy— even if that land is in China, Russia, Sudan, or Korea— their rights and protection are the same as if they were standing on the lawn of the White House in Washington, D.C. The U.S. embassies in those foreign countries are considered to be American soil.

Now picture the reverse. Any time you keep the property of satan's dark empire in your house, you have given him the legal right to establish his presence in your home! In essence, you have given him an embassy. He can send his demons to those islands right in the middle of your home because he has a legal right to operate through whatever property he owns.

With that sobering truth in mind, I encourage you to rid your house of all things that belong to satan. Perhaps you have clipped questionable pictures, articles, or jokes from the magazines, books, or newspapers that enter your home. Maybe some of the trinkets that sit on your tables or shelves, the pictures that grace your walls, or the jewelry that adorns your neck or your spouse's neck have demonic origins. Or you may own Ouija boards, pentagrams, astrological charts, or tarot cards. These things are rooted in the occult. They act like lightning rods for demonic spirits!

As long as the instruments of darkness and the occult are in your house, I guarantee you that they will attract demonic activity. Like draws like. The dark powers that inspire these games, symbols, and tools of divination call to mighty demonic powers in the heavens. They invite them to enter your home, and these powers accept the invitation. Soon green and red streaks run along your walls. You may not notice them, or you may not believe that these things are evil, but this does not change who and what they represent. You have given satan entrance into your house. God sees this even if you do not—or will not. He knows exactly what in your house is causing the pollution. Some things may be hidden. Others are set out on display. Wherever they are, these beacons draw unwelcome and unpleasant company into your home. Get rid of these demonic entrance signs if you are serious about cleansing your sterile home and opening the heavens over your family.

6.   Is satan saddling up the airwaves and riding into your home through the television? Take out all the garbage of ungodly materials that enter your home through the TV set.

In ancient times, the devil was often carried into kingdoms and villages in the form of grand idols that were carried on the shoulders of frenzied worshipers who were willing to sacrifice even their children to him. How he loved these processions that gave him easy access to establish his kingdom in that locale.

In the United States today, many places honor satan once a year with a parade down the main streets of our cities and towns; but satan does not really need golden idols or grand processions to gain access to our homes. He has found an even more effective vehicle for evil. He has found modern media!

Satan is throwing a saddle over the airwaves, locking his feet in the stirrups, and riding right into your home through your television. He lands on your floor and goes to work. Children, in particular, are susceptible to his invasion, since millions of parents have abandoned them to the care of television sets.

I'm not one to advocate blowing up your television. Just control it and watch edifying things. Many parents are not even aware of the potential demonic advance that comes through the inappropriate programs that are available in their homes at the push of a button. Many of these programs contain witchcraft, vulgarity, and obscene material.

I am continually shocked by the filthy and polluted things Christians permit to enter their houses via cable television. Even Lot was able to keep the Sodomites out of his home, but we let them ride the airwaves and other modern media right into our homes with all their filth. Millions of Christian homes are filled with R-rated movies that continually contaminate their environment with repeated mantras of G-- d--- this and s-- o- a b---- that. However, television is not the only media to introduce filth into our homes. Lust-filled movies are also available at any video rental store. Dial-a-sex 900 numbers also pose a significant threat.

Are you hooked on pornography? Do you have a private stash that your kids may have found? Is your teenager secretly using your telephone to access 900 numbers? If you are aware of any ungodly materials that are invading your home, it's time to clean house. There are green and red streaks on your walls.

Start purging your home of the plague that has overcome you. Clean out everything that invites satan's presence and influence in your home. Change your family's future by making the right choices now. Then and only then will your brass skies become clear and your sterile house become fertile. Then and only then, as you rigorously and honestly deal with the sin in your house, can the anointing of God so fill your home and bless your family that you are continually bathed by His loving presence. The heavens are open to those who carefully assess the condition of their homes and take the necessary steps to establish holiness and freedom.

Endnotes

1. See John 5:19.
2. See Matthew 10:21; Romans 1:30.
3. See Exodus 20:8-11.
4. See Luke 14:5.
5. Genesis 27:38.

Chapter 8

Reaping Under an Open Heaven

Before the turn of the century in New York City harbor, all shipping had to pass through a notorious navigation channel called Hell Gate. This passage, which ran between the Bronx and Long Island, was extremely dangerous because of treacherous currents and a cluster of rocks called Flood Rock that jutted up right in the middle of the shipping lane. Even though incoming ship captains approached Hell Gate cautiously, hundreds of ships were destroyed and many lives were lost over the years. It is said that the passage got its name from the old sailors' saying, "Many a godless man has entered hell through that awful gate."

Exasperated city fathers finally brought in engineers to study the problem. In 1885, they placed explosive charges around Flood Rock to blast the obstruction out of the channel and strung the ignition wires all the way through town to the mayor's office at city hall, where they connected them to a switch. The extra effort was made because the event had aroused the population's interest and attracted press attention from around the world.

On October 10th, the mayor and his small daughter met with two witnesses and a group of newspaper reporters and photographers in the mayor's office. After announcing to the press that the switch in his office would detonate the explosive charges that would blast a wider channel through Hell Gate, he suddenly acted on a whim and turned to his little daughter. "Honey, why don't you push the button and set off the blast?" This little girl was thrilled to be with her daddy, but she knew nothing about ships or tides. She was completely ignorant of the technical arrangements and she barely understood what all the fuss was about. But when her father said, "Do it, honey," she obeyed and closed the electrical switch as the reporters watched.

The people who saw the event didn't see any fireworks in the mayor's office that day. They were standing in a building at the heart of the city, far from Hell Gate channel in New York harbor. None of the people in that room saw or heard the explosive eruptions that rocked the harbor immediately after the little girl closed the switch. They simply trusted that all would happen as it had been planned, a trust that was vindicated when the phone rang a few minutes later and an exultant voice on the other end of the line said just five words: "Hell Gate is no more!" To this day, if you drive near New York City harbor, you will see road signs still bearing the name "Hell Gate," but its geographic namesake was destroyed more than a century ago.

A little girl's act of obedience with a dainty finger blasted away the treacherous rocky outcropping that had once taken many lives and blocked the shipping channel into the greatest harbor in the United States. It took only a simple act of childlike obedience to unleash the earth-shattering power that destroyed Hell Gate. Today, God wants to destroy the spiritual gates of hell[1] that still exert great influence on the affairs of men. When we obey Him with the faith of a child, He will release His unlimited power against every ungodly influence that is hardening the brassy skies over our heads and plaguing our homes. This is the miracle and mystery of the cross: Even harlots, thieves, backsliders, and little children can release Heaven's incredible power by repenting, obeying, and submitting to God. It's not *our strength* that moves the stones of bondage entombing our lives; it is the power of Christ released through our humble obedience.

The Gates of Hell Shall Not Prevail

Many Christians have never really grasped what Jesus was saying when He said, "...upon this rock I will build My church; and the *gates of hell* shall not prevail against it."[2] Let's take an in-depth look at "gates" in Scripture. Gates in ancient times were focal points of power.

- *Business* was conducted at the city gates. Boaz took off his shoe and gave it to *the city officials at the gate*, officially indicating that he was redeeming Ruth's possessions.[3]

- *Military strategy* was planned at the gates. It was said that a city would be open and vulnerable if the gates could be taken.[4]

- *Judgments and punishment* were delivered at the gates.[5]

- The husband of a virtuous woman was *known in the gates*.[6]

- Abraham's nephew, Lot, *sat at the gates* of Sodom as an elder.[7]

- The *safety of a city* was determined by the *strength of its gates*. If the enemy stormed the gates and succeeded, his horses, chariots, and machinery of war could then enter.[8]

- *When the gates came down*, the city was conquered.[9]

Right now in the spirit realm, there are evil magistrates, rulers, and elders "sitting at the gates" all over the world plotting, scheming, strategizing, and planning to prevent our churches and our homes from achieving any kind of breakthrough in the heavens. They even craft plans to contaminate businesses and social structures to further their twisted agenda of devilish destruction. Right in the face of this darkness, Jesus, the Light of the world, said that the "gates of hell" would *not* prevail against His Church. They will not prevent, overpower, block, overwhelm, outlast, or win against His Church.

What Is a Gate?

A gate is "an opening in a wall or fence; a city or castle entrance often with defensive structures (as towers); a means of entrance or exit; an area for departure or arrival, a door, valve, or other mechanism for controlling passage; a device that outputs a signal when specified input conditions are met."[10]

Where Are Hell's Gates?

Now that we have defined what a "gate" is, we need to understand what Jesus meant by "hell's gates." The Scriptures describe hell in at least three contexts:

1. *Hell is a literal place or region* in the underworld where God will ultimately incarcerate satan, the fallen angels who followed satan into rebellion, and the souls of humans who chose to reject God's Son as their Savior and Lord.

2. Hell can describe a condition. James 3:6 says,
   And the tongue is a fire, a world of iniquity: so is the tongue among our members, that it defileth the whole body, and setteth on fire the course of nature; and it is set on fire of hell.

   This picture of a tongue that is ignited by the fire of hell also gives us a vivid picture of hell itself.

3. *"Hell's gate" refers to satan's earthly seat of power* as manifested in the brassy *heavens* he creates over the heads of men who consistently disobey God and willfully live in sin. (This does not refer to the gaseous atmosphere surrounding this planet, nor to the high heavens where God Almighty abides on His throne. Satan was cast down from the high heavens.)

Satan is not in hell yet. The Bible says he is the "prince of this world,"[11] and the "prince of the power of the air, the spirit that now worketh in the children of disobedience."[12] He commands the "rulers of the darkness of this world"[13] and he is still on the loose.

In fact, John the apostle told the Church that "...the whole world lieth in [under the power of] wickedness."[14]

So when Jesus talks about the gates of hell, He's not referring to a set of red-hot, smoking, steel-barred gates located in the fire and brimstone dungeons of Hades. That place does indeed exist, and it is waiting for the arrival of the chained serpent and his fallen angels, but it has absolutely no power over the Church. Only its eternally damned inhabitants will suffer it. No, Jesus was not talking about gates in the underworld. He was speaking of devilish gates in the heavens over our heads, where satan the adversary actively works to obstruct the dealings of men with God.

Powers and Principalities in Heavenly Places

The Book of Daniel reveals that satan's "angels" actively work to hinder, steal, or delay God's answers to the prayers of men. While the devil is powerless to hinder, steal from, or delay God, he does have the ability to hinder our prayers *when we let him* do it. Paul the apostle laid out in detail the structure of satan's forces in his Epistle to the Ephesians. One of the first things you should notice is that "powers and principalities" are always used together when referring to satan's dark princedom.

> *For I am persuaded, that neither death, nor life, nor angels, **nor principalities, nor powers**...shall be able to separate us from the love of God, which is in Christ Jesus our Lord* (Romans 8:38-39).

> *To the intent that now unto the **principalities and powers** in heavenly places might be known by the church the manifold wisdom of God* (Ephesians 3:10).

> *For we wrestle not against flesh and blood, but **against principalities, against powers**, against the rulers of the darkness of this world, against spiritual wickedness in high places* (Ephesians 6:12).

> *And having spoiled **principalities and powers**, He made a show of them openly, triumphing over them in it* (Colossians 2:15).

If you study the word *principalities*, you will discover that it comes from the Greek word *arche*, which means "first, beginning, chief, and master."[15] Our modern word *architect* comes from that same Greek root, with the Greek word for "builder" being added. Satan's evil principalities are intelligent architects, builders, and engineers of evil. They study us—our homes, our churches, and our localities—just like an engineer studies topography or structure. Then they craft a scheme or plan, just like an architect designs blueprints for a building or a general lays out battle plans for his troops. Once the plan has been determined, the principalities bring in the "powers, " the devilish muscle, to do the dirty work.

When our church building was being constructed in Pensacola, our architects used to come around from time to time with stacks of plans, blueprints, and schematics. They had envisioned and drawn up the plans for the building to guide the masons, carpenters, plumbers, electricians, and painters who actually did the work. Once we broke ground, I very seldom saw the architects or engineers. They were tucked away downtown somewhere. What I did see every day were the workers. I'd hear the roar of trucks going and coming, the thud of hammers, the hum of saws, and the other noises made by busy laborers who were carrying out the bidding of the architects who were far removed from the actual work.

The *gates of hell* are where the architects and intelligent principalities of satan devise their schemes, plans, and strategies to stop Christians. Their chief goal is to isolate our churches and homes by shutting the heavens over our heads, a task they accomplished by seducing us, tricking us, or persuading us to fall into various sins and acts of disobedience. Wise principalities know the right moves that are needed to distract, discourage, and dishearten us. After they lay the plan, they call in demonic powers to carry out their schemes and plans. Once the battle begins, we had better have our minds made up to persevere, and we'd better be wearing the whole armor of God, because it will be a royal battle! But remember Jesus' promise that the gates of hell *will not prevail*—although they most certainly will assail us!

It is important to realize that you are dealing with *intelligent* schemers and powerful spiritual powers. The kingdom of darkness will pull out all the stops to silence the men or women of God who have an open heaven over their heads. They will do anything to stop the believer who is trying to poke holes in his brassy skies. This is why satan has us under surveillance.

Satan doesn't attack everyone the same way or with the same intensity. In fact, *the devil is not concerned with most Christians.* They are no threat at all because their lives are up and down, in and out, and hot and cold. Their lukewarm walk has pretty well neutralized their effectiveness in the Kingdom of God, so hell doesn't even blink when they get out of bed in the morning! Some people whine and complain to anyone who will listen, "The devil's been on my back all week." No he hasn't! They are not even worthy of a worn-out demon! They are high-maintenance, low-impact Christians who always need pampering, coddling, reassurance, and recognition. Satan's not worried about them at all.

There was one person who attracted the personal attention of the devil himself. After a 40-day fast in the wilderness, this man was confronted by satan himself. He posed such a threat that the devil didn't dare send just any old imp or low-ranking power, or even a principality or a bull demon. The big boy himself came to find out who had such a clear and yielding heaven over His head. He discovered that he was dealing with Jesus Christ, the only begotten Son of God come in the flesh. When, without success, he dangled before the last Adam every temptation he had used to bring down the first Adam, the prince of hell knew that he was in big trouble. The last Adam passed every test with flying colors.

The princedom of hell was in such desperate straits that satan even picked up Jesus and took Him to the pinnacle of the Temple. (How he did it I don't know.) Then the prince of the power of the air offered the Prince of peace all the kingdoms of the world if He would just worship him. All this earned him was a stinging rebuke from God's Word that reminded him who was his Maker and Judge. Jesus moved in absolute obedience and the heavens were pried wide open over His head. By the end of their rendezvous, lucifer knew that his obituary as a free spirit was inevitably written in indestructible stone.

Just as the gates of hell could not prevent, overpower, block, overwhelm, or prevail over Christ in the wilderness or on the cross, neither will they prevail over His blood-washed Church. *But the key is obedience.* An obedient walk before God keeps the heavens open. Nothing satan can do has the power to close them. This is why hell was in a panic over Jesus. Bless the Lord, it's time that snake gets in a panic over this last-day Church!

I want all hell to hear a loud "sucking" sound as such a huge opening in the heavens breaks over Pensacola that angels freely traffic in countless multitudes. I want hell's denizens to tremble as God's anointing sizzles, His glory falls, revival fire races, miraculous healings crackle, and mighty deliverances explode one after another!

I know the Scriptures say that evil will get worse and worse, and I believe that the events of the end times are still on schedule, but God said that *when sin abounds, His grace abounded much more.*[16] We've tried everything this world and satan have to offer, but they've only left us empty. We rode the beast of religion until it dumped us off in a desert, so dry and defeated that we were almost dead. Praise God, we had just enough life left in us that we could be resuscitated and revived. While we lay in that desert, panting, disoriented, and desperate, *God sent a river*!

When the tide comes in along a seacoast, it lifts *all* boats. Whether they are huge ocean-going liners stuck in sandbars or tiny shrimp boats beached above the waterline, the tide lifts them all. The tide of God's glory is rolling in. Watch out, satan! We are coming after your gates, and we are going to strip you of your plans, schemes, and blueprints. Hell's powers and muscle are no match for the redeemed saints of God who are endued with the power of the Holy Ghost. One of us can put a thousand to flight, and two can put ten thousand to flight![17] What an amortization plan!

God's people are getting straightened out. They are repenting and turning from sin and disobedience. They are waking up, lining up, and suiting up for battle. I believe that some of the greatest exploits in the Kingdom are right before us. Take courage, saints! God's Word promises us even more than the power to prevail:

> *Thus saith the Lord to His anointed, to Cyrus, whose right hand I have holden, to subdue nations before him; and **I will loose the loins of kings,** to open before him the two leaved gates; and the gates shall not be shut; I will go before thee, and make the crooked places straight: **I will break in pieces the gates of brass,** and cut in sunder the bars of iron: And I will **give thee the treasures of darkness, and hidden riches of secret places,** that thou mayest know that I, the Lord, which call thee by thy name, am the God of Israel* (Isaiah 45:1-3).

God said some very important things to Cyrus, the king of Persia. He said that He would cause a king (King Belshazzar of Babylon) to open the two-leaved gates and those gates would not be shut. He said that He would break up the gates of brass and cut apart the bars of iron. Then God said that He would give Cyrus the treasures of darkness and the hidden riches of secret places. What a powerful Scripture!

I realize that this Scripture passage was literally fulfilled when the armies of King Cyrus led by Darius the Mede invaded Babylon and captured it in one night. But this event from Daniel's day also contains a great spiritual truth. God had used the Babylonian empire to punish Israel for its apostasy and idolatry. Their national sin had opened them up to spiritual and physical captivity. All the riches of Jerusalem were plundered and carried away to the hidden treasure houses of Babylon. Her finest young men and women were stolen away to serve ungodly kings in a distant land. Even her Temple of worship and sacrifice was destroyed and the national identity of the Jews was eliminated. Still, even after decades of captivity, there was a longing in the hearts of God's people for a homeland and a wondrous reunion with their God.

In answer to their prayers, God raised up Cyrus to conquer the mighty Babylonian empire. Once this had happened, Cyrus released the Jews to return to their homeland, exactly as God prophesied through Isaiah. Then He moved on the Persian king of Nehemiah's day to allow the Jews to rebuild Jerusalem and restore her walls. Without the Jews raising even one weapon of war, God sovereignly moved to deliver His captive nation by raising up one empire to destroy another. The Jews' part in this affair was to obey.

Where Are My Goods, Devil?

Have you ever asked yourself, "Am I *missing* something? Where are the things satan has stolen from me?" These stolen things are *still in existence* somewhere, even though you can't see them. When satan steals our blessings, he doesn't destroy them because he doesn't have the power or authority to do so. He locks away these "treasures of darkness, and hidden riches of secret places."

What then are these treasures and riches? We know from God's Word that "every good gift and every perfect gift is from above, and cometh down from the Father of lights, with whom is no variableness, neither shadow of turning."[18] How are these treasures of darkness different from the gifts and treasures of God, who is light?

These stolen and hidden goods are *our treasures*. They are "treasures of darkness" because the enemy has tucked them away in the secret treasure chests of his dark realm. Satan stole them by keeping our blessings from us, but God wants to give them back. Therefore He promises to "break in pieces the gates of brass, and cut in sunder the bars of iron." God is plundering satan's treasure chests to restore what was seized by theft and deception.

Satan locked up the treasures of Daniel and Israel by brassing over the heavens above their heads, but Daniel's 24 days of persistent prayer brought heavenly action. An angel appeared to Daniel and said,

> ...*Fear not, Daniel: for from the first day that thou didst set thine heart to understand, and to chasten thyself before thy God, **thy words were heard**...* (Daniel 10:12).

God heard Daniel immediately, but Daniel still had to persevere in prayer until he saw the angel appear and say:

...I am come for thy words (Daniel 10:12).

Beginning in Daniel 10:12, the Scriptures show how the angel pulled aside the veil that separates the realm of flesh from that of eternal spirit. He gave Daniel keen insight into the battles of heavenly princes and the crucial role our prayers play in their outcomes.

Four Results of Daniel's Prayers

1. His prayer brought heavenly action.

Every child of God should be excited when he sees that Daniel's prayers were heard and acted upon the *first day* he fell to his knees and prayed. *Every single prayer offered in obedience and purity is heard and answered by God!*[19] These answers are not always immediately visible, however, because God has ordained that some answers, like the dispatching of the angel to Daniel, will be brought to fulfillment by fervent unyielding prayer.

2. It unlocked information.

Daniel learned vital information in four areas—the future of the Jewish people, the power of his prayer and the instant response God gave it, the nature of spiritual warfare in the heavenlies, and God's opinion of him as an individual.[20]

The angel gave Daniel one of the Bible's most far-reaching and detailed prophecies concerning future world events. The prophecy covers a large segment of Middle Eastern and Western world history, including the conquests of Alexander the Great, Artexerxes, Antiochus Epiphanes (who profaned the Temple in Jerusalem), and the Roman Empire.

3. It unlocked angelic help.

The warrior-prince from heaven told Daniel, "I am come for thy words."[21] It was Daniel's prayer that provoked the divine dispatch of angelic force and support for Daniel and his nation. It was his *continuing prayer* that unleashed the formidable power of

Michael, the archangel who assisted in bringing to Daniel God's answer to his prayer. Daniel's prayer literally unleashed the hounds of heaven on the demonic prince of Persia.

Please note, these heavenly beings were not like the tame variety of angels we usually imagine. The angel told Daniel,

...now will I return to fight with the prince of Persia (Daniel 10:20a).

That Hebrew word, *lacham*, literally means "to feed on; to consume (figuratively), to devour, overcome, prevail."[22] Daniel was in the presence of a very warlike angel who fought to win!

4. It unlocked supernatural strength.

At the time of the angel's appearing, Daniel was already weakened by 21 days of partial fast and constant intercessory prayer over his heartbreaking burden. The appearance and voice of the angel caused him to faint, thereby making him unable to receive the angelic message. Part of the angel's assignment was to strengthen the man of God, just as angels ministered to Jesus after His 40-day fast and His confrontation with the devil. The angel touched Daniel's body three times as he imparted new strength to him.[23]

Daniel moved kings, nations, and demonic principalities from his knees. We can only imagine what he might have done had he lived on this side of the cross! Demonic strategy continues at hell's gates, but Jesus declared those gates powerless against His Church. This is guaranteed by Christ's birth, death, and resurrection, and His gift of the Holy Spirit to the Church.

Nevertheless, you and I have a part to play in God's plan. Let's try to better understand our role by looking at two powerful Scriptures concerning gates:

*That **in blessing I will bless thee**, and in multiplying I will multiply thy seed as the stars of the heaven, and as the sand which is upon the sea shore; and **thy seed shall possess the gate of his enemies*** (Genesis 22:17).

*In that day shall the Lord of hosts be for a crown of glory, and for a diadem of beauty, unto the residue of His people, and for a spirit of judgment to him that sitteth in judgment, and **for strength to them that turn the battle to the gate*** (Isaiah 28:5-6).

God is interested in action based on obedience. If we will *turn the battle to hell's gate*, He will supply the strength for the battle! The devil has been busy making the heavens brass by getting us to live in sin and disobedience. Then he stole our most precious treasures and locked them away. He has been especially slick in his campaign against the Church. While the Church has squabbled, entertained, griped, and slept its way to needless failure by being distracted by things that are irrelevant, he has orchestrated and schemed planned attacks.

The Tide Is Turning

This will no more be true! From all the signs, the tide is turning. The Church is repenting and getting on fire for God. We now have seen over 100,000 decisions for Christ in Brownsville Assembly of God since June of 1995, and the number grows daily. We are determined to retrieve the treasures of darkness that satan has locked away behind gates of brass. We are demanding that he return all the hidden riches he has stashed in secret places. We are requiring the immediate return of all satan has stolen: our rest, our peace, our joy, our blessings, our happy homes, our children, our ministries and anointing, and our health and well-being.

Satan Is Nervous

I have a feeling that satan is becoming quite nervous about this last-day awakening. I have personally seen some people recently come to Jesus who had never experienced peace, joy, or true rest until they were saved. Now they are red-hot mad at the devil, and believe me, they are violent! They are coming after their lost treasures, and they are confronting satan himself.

I've heard them testify from our baptismal pool on Friday evenings. I've listened to their tales of past woe, misery, and anguish. They know that they have been robbed and they are extremely angry! I believe that satan is about to have his loot spoiled, for he will lose his stolen treasures right before the coming of Christ! Despite every effort of hell, the revival of God is not diminishing. Every day the numbers are growing. We are seeing "the chiefest of sinners" run to the altar to receive Christ as Lord. By the hundreds they stream forward night after night to repent and get right with God. When they leave the altar, they are itching for battle with the one who has robbed them blind.

It's going to be interesting to see all the losses hell will take in coming days! The New Testament account reveals that Jesus was *ruthless* with the devil and his crew. The Lord stayed on the cross and tenaciously held out until He knocked the crown from satan's head. He persevered until He had personally invaded the underworld, preached to the captives, and snatched the keys of death and hell from lucifer's trembling grip.

Jesus took the arrows of death and broke them in half, giving only the feathered part back. He forever removed the sting of death for His saints, and He did it through obedience. Jesus Christ spoiled the devil's powers and principalities, making "a show of them openly."[24] Jesus had no mercy. He taunted, mocked, and defanged that old serpent right in front of his duped followers and former captives. Jesus was merciless. If you think He had a tantrum when He spilled the take of the money changers, just imagine what He did when He openly made a show of satan!

Some people in the Church have slow-danced with the devil over the last few years. But friends, there is a new crowd out there that will have nothing to do with compromise. They are a new breed of believers. They have fire in their eyes and swords in their hands. God has poured out His mighty river and the Church will never be the same.

Centuries ago, Jesus told Peter and the disciples,
*And I will give unto thee **the keys of the kingdom** of heaven* (Matthew 16:19a).
Believe me, this new crowd is storming hell's gates, and they are doing more than binding and loosing. They are all over hell's case! They just aren't interested in the halfway measures of Joash:

And Elisha said unto [King Joash], Take bow and arrows. And he took unto him bow and arrows. And he said to the king of Israel, Put thine hand upon the bow. And he put his hand upon it: and Elisha put his hands upon the king's hands. And he said, Open the window eastward. And he opened it. Then Elisha said, Shoot. And he shot. And he said, The arrow of the Lord's deliverance, and the arrow of deliverance from Syria: for **thou shalt smite the Syrians in Aphek, till thou have consumed them.** *And he said, Take the arrows. And he took them. And he said unto the king of Israel,* **Smite upon the ground.** *And* **he smote thrice, and stayed. And the man of God was wroth with him,** *and said, Thou shouldest have smitten five or six times; then hadst thou smitten Syria till thou hadst consumed it: whereas now thou shalt smite Syria but thrice* (2 Kings 13:15-19).

Elisha opened a window eastward toward Syria, the direction from which the attack would come. Then the prophet put his hand on Joash, signifying that the source of prophetic authority, the Holy Spirit, was empowering Joash to shoot the arrow toward Syria. After clearly telling Joash that God wanted him to totally destroy the Syrian army, Elisha told the king to strike the ground with the arrows. When Joash only struck the ground three times, Elisha was angry over the king's timidity in war. In essence he said, "You should have struck the ground five or six times. Then you would have battled with Syria until you had totally destroyed it. Now you will defeat Syria only three times. Then watch out!"

In my mind's eye, I can see this generation pointing a handful of God's arrows directly toward the heavens of brass and the treasures of darkness. I can almost hear the Holy Spirit saying, "Shoot! Now strike the ground!" This new generation isn't bashful, ashamed, or intimidated. The tide of God's glory is rising. Abandon your brassy gates, satan! We are coming after your gates, your plans, your schemes, and your blueprints. We are determined to bind you and to totally despoil your house! We've been robbed and cheated; now we are out for righteous revenge! This time we have the unlimited power of Heaven behind us! It is written in the Book and sealed in Jesus' blood.

Satan,
You can't prevail.
You have to open the two-leaved gates!
You can't shut the gates anymore as long as we obey the King.
God Himself is breaking your gates of brass.
He has cut your bars of iron in pieces.
God has promised us every treasure of darkness.
You must reveal and release every bit of our hidden riches
that you have stored in secret places!

This angry generation of redeemed sinners is striking the ground again and again with holy violence. They will settle for nothing less than complete and absolute victory over their enemy! They are utterly ruthless with the devil, just like their new Master. There's a swirl of dust arising from every quarter of America where sinners have recently been snatched from hell's gate, as a brand is taken from the burning fire! These new believers are bent on revenge. They are moving headlong into the enemy's camp and taking back *all* that the devil stole from them.

It's a joy to see God raising up such a powerful new band of mighty warriors with no religion in them to stifle them. As the Holy Ghost helps them and works with them they are boldly daring to do last-day exploits. The Spirit of God is thrilled to see this righteous crew the Father is raising up to raze and tear down the gates of hell. I'd love to see the Church rise up in a battle frenzy as we violently turn back the battle toward the gates of hell. May we soon hear the words ring out, *"The gates of hell are no more!"*

Endnotes

1. The author acknowledges his indebtedness to Dick Bernal's discussion of hell's gates in *Storming Hell's Brazen Gates* (San Jose, CA: Jubilee Christian Center, 1988).
2. Matthew 16:18.
3. See Ruth 4:1-11.
4. See Obadiah 1:11.

5. See Deuteronomy 17:5.
6. Proverbs 31:23.
7. See Genesis 19:1.
8. See 2 Chronicles 14:7.
9. See Nehemiah 1:3.
10. *Merriam Webster's Collegiate Dictionary,* p. 482.
11. John 16:11.
12. Ephesians 2:2.
13. Ephesians 6:12.
14. 1 John 5:19.
15. *Strong's,* **arche** (Gr., #746).
16. See Romans 5:20.
17. See Deuteronomy 32:30.
18. James 1:17.
19. See John 15:16; 16:23-24.
20. See Daniel 10:10-12; 12:13.
21. Daniel 10:12b.
22. *Strong's,* **fight** (Heb. #3898).
23. See Daniel 10:10,16,18.
24. Colossians 2:15.

Destiny Image
Revival Books